MW01221685

# Japanese Grammar for Beginners
# Textbook + Workbook Included

## Supercharge Your Japanese With Essential Lessons and Exercises

**Also available:**

- Japanese Short Stories for Beginners (https://geni.us/japanesestores1)

# Table of contents

# Introduction

When learning any language, grammar definitely comes up as the most challenging—and boring—part. Japanese is no different. Unfortunately, grammar is not something that can just be brushed off as an afterthought.

You simply cannot skip learning grammar if you truly want to become proficient. It doesn't work that way, and there are no shortcuts. If you want to be able to express yourself in Japanese using clear and precise language, you need to build a solid foundation in Japanese grammar.

This book is here to help you. In the lessons in this book, we will lay down the rules in Japanese grammar and provide you with lots of examples, clarifications, and exercises.

## Practice Your Japanese Listening Skills and Pronunciation

A key to success in language learning is to get a good grasp of pronunciation at the beginning of your lessons. This requires constant listening practice. With this book's audio accompaniment, you will get a headstart in your listening comprehension as well as hone your pronunciation straight off the bat.

Each lesson and exercise contains audio narrated by a native Japanese speaker. By listening to the audio and reading the written text at the same time, you will be able to connect how a word and sentence looks with how it sounds when spoken in actual Japanese conversations.

## Embedded Grammar Workbook

There is no need to buy a separate workbook to help you practice the grammar points you learn. We have integrated different types of exercises into the book. This way, you will be able to cement your learning through taking the quizzes after each grammar lesson and you will be able to assess your progress as you go along.

## Build a Learning Habit

This book also aims to help you build a learning habit that will help you sustain your Japanese learning even if your motivation wanes as you go along. You'll find that the book is divided into 17 lessons, with one lesson meant to be tackled each day. After 17 days of studying consistently everyday, you will have formed a learning habit that will ultimately help you achieve your learning goals.

## Japanese Grammar, Simplified

Japanese grammar is already complicated—we don't need to make it even more complex. So in this book, you'll notice that we use the simplest yet thorough explanations. We do not want to burden you with wordy explanations and unnecessary jargon. Instead, in this book we explain Japanese grammar in a way that makes it easily digestible and easy to grasp.

We have put a lot of effort into this book so that it will be most useful to your Japanese language learning journey. We certainly hope that it will help you build the strong grammar foundation you need to eventually reach fluency in Japanese .

Thank you very much.

Frederic Bibard

Founder, Talk in Japanese

**Important! The link to download the Audio Files is available at the end of this book. (Page 283)**

# Lesson 1: Getting your tongue around Japanese – a pronunciation guide

In this lesson, you will learn:

- How to read romaji
- How to read & write hiragana
- How to read & write katakana
- Pronunciation tips

## Writing

### A little bit about the Japanese writing system

In order to learn how to pronounce Japanese we ought to look a little bit at its writing system.

The Japanese writing system uses a mix of different types of characters: hiragana ひらがな, katakana カタカナ, and kanji 漢字. They are usually learned in that order.

In this section, though, we will be focusing on how to actually say the syllables.

The sounds are represented by 46 characters not including the blends or the existing syllables modified with the small circle or two quotation-like marks.

For example, は (*ha*) becomes ば (*ba*) if you add two quotation-like marks, and ぱ (*pa*) if you add a small circle to the upper right of the character.

### *Listen to tracks 1 and 2*

| Hiragana | Katakana | Romaji | Pronunciation | Example |
|---|---|---|---|---|
| あ | ア | *a* | *ah* | ありがとう *arigatou* (thank you) |
| い | イ | *i* | *ee* | イギリス *igirisu* (U.K.) |
| う | ウ | *u* | *oo* | うさぎ *usagi* (rabbit) |
| え | エ | *e* | *eh* | えいご *eigo* (English language) |
| お | オ | *o* | *oh* | おにぎり *onigiri* (rice ball) |
| か | カ | *ka* | *kah* | かみ *kami* (hair/paper) |
| き | キ | *ki* | *kee* | きめる *kimeru* (decide) |
| く | ク | *ku* | *koo* | くるま *kuruma* (car) |

| け | ケ | ke | keh | ケーキ *keeki* (cake) |
|---|---|---|---|---|
| こ | コ | ko | koh | ここ *koko* (here) |
| が | ガ | ga | gah | ガム *gamu* (gum) |
| ぎ | ギ | gi | gee | ぎん *gin* (silver) |
| ぐ | グ | gu | goo | グループ *guruupu* (group) |
| げ | ゲ | ge | geh | げか *geka* (surgery) |
| ご | ゴ | go | goh | ごま *goma* (sesame) |
| さ | サ | sa | sah | さしみ *sashimi* |
| し | シ | shi/si | shee | しぬ *shinu* (die) |
| す | ス | su | soo | すし *sushi* |
| せ | セ | se | seh | せんせい *sensei* (teacher) |
| そ | ソ | so | soh | その *sono* (that) |
| ざ | ザ | za | zah | さいご *saigo* (last) |
| じ | ジ | ji | jee | じかん *jikan* (time) |
| ず | ズ | zu | zoo | ずっと *zutto* (the whole time) |
| ぜ | ゼ | ze | zeh | ぜったい *zettai* (definitely) |
| ぞ | ゾ | zo | zoh | ぞう *zou* (elephant) |
| た | タ | ta | tah | たたみ *tatami* |
| ち | チ | chi | chee | ちいさい *chiisai* (small) |
| つ | ツ | tsu | tsu | つき *tsuki* (moon) |
| て | テ | te | teh | テリヤキ *teriyaki* |
| と | ト | to | toh | とら *tora* (tiger) |
| だ | ダ | da | dah | だいがく *daigaku* (university) |
| ぢ | ヂ | ji/di/dzi | jee | ちぢむ *chijimu* |
| づ | ヅ | zu/du/dzu | dzoo | つちづくり *tsuchizukuri* (maintaining the soil) |
| で | デ | de | deh | でる *deru* (go out/come out) |
| ど | ド | do | doh | どうが *douga* (video) |
| な | ナ | na | nah | なる *naru* (become) |
| に | ニ | ni | nii | にんげん *ningen* (human) |
| ぬ | ヌ | nu | noo | ぬる *nuru* (paint) |

| ね | ネ | ne | neh | ねる *neru* (sleep) |
|---|---|---|---|---|
| の | ノ | no | noh | のる *noru* (ride) |
| ま | マ | ma | mah | まる *maru* (circle) |
| み | ミ | mi | mee | みる *miru* (watch) |
| む | ム | mu | moo | むし *mushi* (insect) |
| め | メ | me | meh | メガネ *megane* (glasses) |
| も | モ | mo | moh | もり *mori* (forest) |
| は | ハ | ha | hah | はい *hai* (yes) |
| ひ | ヒ | hi | hee | ひまわり *himawari* (sunflower) |
| ふ | フ | fu/hu | fuu | ふたり *futari* (two people) |
| へ | ヘ | he | heh | へる *heru* (decrease) |
| ほ | ホ | ho | hoh | ほし *hoshi* (star) |
| や | ヤ | ya | yah | やめる *yameru* (quit) |
| よ | ヨ | yo | yoh | よむ *yomu* (read) |
| ゆ | ユ | yu | yu | ゆめ *yume* (dream) |
| わ | ワ | wa | wa | わたし *watashi* (I/me) |
| を | ヲ | wo | oh | ほん　を　よむ *hon wo yomu* (read books) |
| ん | ン | n | n | きん *kin* (gold) |
| ら | ラ | ra | rah | らいしゅう *raishuu* (next week) |
| り | リ | ri | ree | りんご *ringo* (apple) |
| る | ル | ru | roo | ルーム *ruumu* (room) |
| れ | レ | re | reh | れんしゅう *renshuu* (practice) |
| ろ | ロ | ro | roh | ロボット *robotto* (robot) |

## Blends

By combining smaller versions of some of the syllables, you get blends.

They can be tricky to say as well as to hear as they can sound similar to each other.

For example, りょ (*ryo*) and りよ (*riyo*) sound very similar, but are pronounced slightly differently, with the former requiring the syllables to be slurred together, whereas each syllable is pronounced separately in the latter.

## Listen to tracks 3 and 4

| Hiragana | Katakana | Pronunciation/ Romaji | Example |
|---|---|---|---|
| きゃ | キャ | kya | キャラメル *kyarameru* (caramel) |
| きゅ | キュ | kyu | きゅうに *kyuuni* (suddenly) |
| きょ | キョ | kyo | きょうみ *kyoumi* (interest) |
| しゃ | シャ | sha | しゃしん *shashin* (photo) |
| しゅ | シュ | shu | しゅみ *shumi* (hobby) |
| しょ | ショ | sho | しょうかい *shoukai* (introduce) |
| ちゃ | チャ | cha | ちゃわん *chawan* (rice bowl) |
| ちゅ | チュ | chu | ちゅうしゃ *chuusha* (parking) |
| ちょ | チョ | cho | ちょうちょう *chouchou* (butterfly) |
| にゃ | ニャ | nya | にゃんこ *nyanko* (kitty) |
| にゅ | ニュ | nyu | ニュース *nyuusu* (news) |
| にょ | ニョ | nyo | ニョロニョロ *nyoronyoro* (slithering [onomatopoeia]) |
| ひゃ | ヒャ | hya | ひゃく *hyaku* (hundred) |
| ひゅ | ヒュ | hyu | ひゅう *hyuu* (wind blowing [onomatopoeia]) |
| ひょ | ヒョ | hyo | ひょっこり *hyokkori* (by chance) |
| みゃ | ミャ | mya | みゃく *myaku* (pulse) |
| みゅ | ミュ | myu | ミュージカル *myuujikaru* (musical) |
| みょ | ミョ | myo | みょうじ *myouji* (surname) |
| りゃ | リャ | rya | りゃくご *ryakugo* (abbreviation) |
| りゅ | リュ | ryu | りゅう *ryuu* (dragon) |
| りょ | リョ | ryo | りょうかい *ryoukai* (OK/roger) |
| ぎゃ | ギャ | gya | ぎゃく *gyaku* (opposite) |
| ぎゅ | ギュ | gyu | ぎゅうにゅう *gyuunyuu* (milk) |
| ぎょ | ギョ | gyo | ぎょうざ *gyouza* |
| じゃ | ジャ | ja | じゃき *jyaki* (evil) |
| じゅ | ジュ | ju | じゅんび *junbi* (preparations) |
| じょ | ジョ | jo | じょせい *josei* (woman) |
| びゃ | ビャ | bya | びゃくい *byakui* (white clothing) |
| びゅ | ビュ | byu | ビューティー *byuutii* (beauty) |
| びょ | ビョ | byo | びょういん *byouin* (hospital) |
| ぴゃ | ピャ | pya | はっぴゃく *happyaku* (eight hundred) |

| ぴゅ | ピュ | pyu | ピュア pyua (pure) |
| ぴょ | ピョ | pyo | ぴょんぴょん pyonpyon (jumping [onomatopoeia]) |

## The — syllable

When you see the — syllable it means you need to lengthen the previous vowel sound.

This syllable is often used when writing non-Japanese names in katakana.

## Examples:

### Listen to track 5

jenii (Jenny) ジェニー

harii (Harry) ハリー

keeki (cake) ケーキ

merii kurisumasu (Merry Christmas) メリークリスマス

## Double consonants

Double consonants are represented by a small version of つ like this っ or in katakana like this ッ.

## Examples:

### Listen to track 6

hotto suru ほっとする

hotto keeki ホットケーキ

## Making non-Japanese sounds

### Listen to track 7

Small versions of the characters can be used to create sounds that don't exist in Japanese language such as ディ di, ファ fa, ヴィ vi.

## Examples:

harouiin ハロウィーン halloween

fasshon ファッション fashion

*vikutorii* ヴィクトリー victory

*paatii* パーティー party

*firipin* フィリピン Philippines

## Watch out for exceptions!

### *Listen to track 8*

Some hiragana syllables are pronounced differently when acting as "particles" in a sentence.

One of these particles is は, which is generally pronounced "*hah*," but when it is acting as a particle, it is pronounced "*wah*."

## Example:

I am an American. (*watashi wa amerikajin desu.*) (わたし は アメリカじん です。)

Another exception is へ which is pronounced "*heh*," but when it is acting as a particle, it is pronounced "*eh*."

## Extra tips

1. When pronouncing the "R" sound in Japanese, it is not the same "R" that you know. Your mouth makes the movement of "L," while voicing an "R" sound. It sounds tricky, but if you listen to Japanese people saying it, it is easier to grasp the sound you should be trying to make.
2. "F" sounds are also a little different from an English speaker's idea of "F." The Japanese "F" is like a mixture of "F" and "H," which is why you occasionally see the words romanized with an H. If you try to make an "F" sound as you usually would, but avoid biting down on your lip completely – as though your teeth are just "in the way" – and say "hoo," you should successfully make the Japanese "F."
3. The nasal "G" is a sound that is good to recognize, but the number of people using it is decreasing with each generation, but here are some times when you would hear the nasal "G" from those who use it.

Use the nasal "G" for the particle *ga* (が).

Use the nasal "G" for almost all "G" sounds that are not at the beginning of the word.

Example: *ongaku* (おんがく).

## Exceptions for the nasal "G" sound

### *Listen to track 9*

1. Use the hard "G" for onomatopoeia words with "G."
2. Example: *gorogoro* (ゴロゴロ).
3. Use the hard "G" for loanwords that are not of Chinese origin.
4. Example: *orugan* (オルガン) organ, *kiroguramu* (キログラム) kilogram
5. Use the hard "G" for number "5" – *go* (五).
6. When a *ga* sound has the honorific "o" (お) before it, use the hard "G."
7. Example: *o-genki* (おげんき), *o-guai* (おぐあい), etc.

## The kana

We looked at the kana – hiragana and katakana – earlier in this unit.

The characters have a specific stroke order which should be followed when writing as you can see below.

# Lesson activities

## Exercise 1

Write the hiragana for these syllables.

1. *hi* _____
2. *yo* _____
3. *ma* _____
4. *re* _____
5. *ku* _____

6. *a* _____
7. *shi* _____
8. *te* _____
9. *n* _____
10. *wo* _____

## Exercise 2

Write the katakana for these syllables.

1. *ki* _____
2. *o* _____
3. *su* _____
4. *tsu* _____
5. *ne* _____

6. *mu* _____
7. *he* _____
8. *ya* _____
9. *ra* _____
10. *wa* _____

## Answer key

## Exercise 1

Write the hiragana for these syllables.

1. *hi* ひ
2. *yo* よ
3. *ma* ま
4. *re* れ
5. *ku* く

6. *a* あ
7. *shi* し
8. *te* て
9. *n* ん
10. *wo* を

## Exercise 2

Write the katakana for these syllables.

1. *ki* キ
2. *o* オ
3. *su* ス
4. *tsu* ツ
5. *ne* ネ

6. *mu* ム
7. *he* ヘ
8. *ya* ヤ
9. *ra* ラ
10. *wa* ワ

Here we will look at the Japanese number system. If you are familiar with the Chinese counting system, you may notice some similarities. The Japanese number system has some tricky readings, but with some practice, you are sure to start recognizing which reading is required.

In this lesson, you will learn:

- Numbers 0-10
- How to form larger numbers
- Counters
- Basic math terminology

## Vocabulary

### The basic numbers

Here are the basic 0-10 numbers that will be the building blocks that you need to know to make the larger numbers later in this lesson.

When handling money, there are 1 yen, 5 yen, and 10 yen coins.

*__Listen to track 10__*

| Number | Kanji | On-reading | Kun-reading | Most commonly used reading |
|--------|-------|------------|-------------|----------------------------|
| 0 | 零 | *rei/zero* | - | *zero* |
| 1 | 一 | *ichi* | *hitotsu* | *ichi* |
| 2 | 二 | *ni* | *futatsu* | *ni* |
| 3 | 三 | *san* | *mittsu* | *san* |
| 4 | 四 | *shi* | *yottsu/yon/yo* | *yon* |
| 5 | 五 | *go* | *itsutsu* | *go* |
| 6 | 六 | *roku* | *muttsu* | *roku* |
| 7 | 七 | *shichi* | *nanatsu/nana* | *nana* |
| 8 | 八 | *hachi* | *yattsu* | *hachi* |
| 9 | 九 | *kyuu/ku* | *kokonotsu* | *kyuu* |
| 10 | 十 | *juu* | *too/to/tou* | *juu* |

## A little quiz

### Exercise 1

Write these words as numerals.

1. *san* _____
2. *shichi* _____
3. *juu* _____

4. *ichi* _____
5. *hachi* _____
6. *go* _____

### Answers key

Write these words as numerals.

1. *san* 3
2. *shichi* 7
3. *juu* 10

4. *ichi* 1
5. *hachi* 8
6. *go* 5

### Exercise 2

Write these numbers as *romaji*.

1. 2 _____
2. 9 _____
3. 0 _____

4. 4 _____
5. 6 _____
6. 10 _____

### Answers key

Write these numbers as *romaji*.

1. 2 *ni*
2. 9 *kyuu*
3. 0 *rei / zero*

4. 4 *yon / shi*
5. 6 *roku*
6. 10 *juu*

## Culture corner

### Why two versions?

A huge number of Chinese words were adopted and integrated into Japanese, including the Chinese numbers. The Chinese reading for numbers is known as *onyomi* (音読み、おんよみ) and these readings are used for numbering most things, like counting, months, and time. There are, however, four numbers where the Japanese *kunyomi* are used: one *hi* ひ, two *fu* ふ, four *yon* よん, and seven *nana* なな.

11

Here are some examples of how to use the different readings.

## 4 - *yon / shi*

### Listen to track 11

The number 4 is read as yon when referring to someone's age.

よんさい *yonsai* four years old

The number 4 is also read as *yon* when using big numbers.

よんじゅう *yonjuu* 40
よんひゃく *yonhyaku* 400
よんせん *yonsen* 4,000
よんまん *yonman* 40,000
よんじゅうまん *yonjuuman* 400,000

But you have to use *shi* for month of April.

しがつ *shigatsu* April

Sometimes 4 is also read as "yo" to make the word easier to say.

よじ *yoji* 4 o'clock
よにん *yonin* four people
じゅうよにん *juuyonin* fourteen people

## 7 - *nana / shichi*

### Listen to track 12

*nana* is also used in ages:
ななさい *nanasai* 7 years old
じゅうななさい *juunanasai* 17 years old
ななじゅっさい *nanajussai* 70 years old

*nana* is used with big numbers:
ななじゅう *nanajuu* 70

ななひゃく *nanahyaku* 700

ななせん *nanasen* 7,000

ななまん *nanaman* 70,000

However, for the month and … o'clock, *shichi* is used:

しちがつ *shichigatsu* July

しちじ *shichiji* 7 o'clock

## 9 - *kyuu / ku*

The number 9 is generally said as *kyuu*, but 9 o'clock is one common exception:

### *Listen to track 13*

くじ *kuji* nine o'clock

# The counting units

Just as we use "a piece of," "a slice of," or "a bunch of," the Japanese language also uses counters.

## The most useful counters

The most important two to remember are 一つ **(kun reading number + *tsu*)** and 一個 **(commonly used reading number + *ko*)**.

Even if you don't remember how to say any of the other counters, you will be understood perfectly with these two counters. However, it is useful to be able to recognize the other counters when you hear them.

## Counters that you need to know

Some of these have some tricky readings, so watch out!

### *Listen to track 14*

## 本　*(hon/bon/pon)* counter for long and thin items

*sooseeji ippon* ソーセージ　いっぽん one sausage

*enpitsu nihon* えんぴつ　にほん　two pencils

*pen sanbon* ぺん　さんぼん three pens

*sooseeji yonhon* ソーセージ　よんほん four sausages

*enpitsu gohon* えんぴつ　ごほん　five pencils

*pen roppon* ぺん　ろっぽん six pens

*sooseeji nanahon* ソーセージ　ななほん seven sausages

*enpitsu happon* えんぴつ　はっぽん　eight pencils

*pen kyuuhon* ぺん　きゅうほん nine pens

*sooseeji juppon* ソーセージ　じゅっぽん ten sausages

## Listen to track 15

## 枚　*(mai)* counter for flat items

*kami ichimai* かみ　いちまい one piece of paper

*kaado nimai* カード　にまい　two cards

*CD sanmai* シーディー　さんまい three CDs

*kami yonmai* かみ　よんまい four pieces of paper

*kaado gomai* カード　ごまい five cards

*CD rokumai* シーディー　ろくまい six CDs

*kami nanamai* かみ　ななまい seven pieces of paper

*kaado hachimai* カード　はちまい eight cards

*CD kyuumai* シーディー　きゅうまい nine CDs

*kami juumai* かみ　じゅうまい ten pieces of paper

## Listen to track 16

## 匹　*(hiki/biki/piki)* counter for animals

*neko ippiki* ネコ　いっぴき one cat

*inu nihiki* いぬ　にひき two dogs

*hamusutaa sanbiki* ハムスター　さんびき three hamsters

*neko yonhiki* ネコ　よんひき four cats

*inu gohiki* いぬ　ごひき two dogs

*hamusutaa roppiki* ハムスター　ろっぴき six hamsters

*neko nanahiki* ネコ　ななひき seven cats

*inu happiki* いぬ　はっぴき eight dogs

*hamusutaa kyuuhiki* ハムスター　きゅうひき nine hamsters

*neko juppiki* ネコ　じゅっぴき ten cats

## Listen to track 17

頭 *(tou)* counter for large animals, rare animals, working animals, and animals in facilities

*zou ittou* ぞう　いっとう one elephant

*chinpanjii nitou* チンパンジー　にとう two chimpanzees

*gorira santou* ゴリラ　さんとう three gorillas

*saru yontou* サル　よんとう four monkeys

*panda gotou* パンダ　ごとう　five pandas

*hitsuji rokutou* ひつじ　ろくとう six sheep

*buta nanatou* ぶた　ななとう seven pigs

*ushi hattou* うし　はっとう eight cows

*ookami kyuutou* おおかみ　きゅうとう nine wolves

*inu juttou* いぬ　じゅっとう ten dogs

## Listen to track 18

羽 *(wa)* counter for birds, bats, and rabbits

*usagi ichiwa* ウサギ　いちわ one rabbit

*usagi niwa* ウサギ　にわ two rabbits

*usagi sanwa* ウサギ　さんわ three rabbits

*usagi yonwa* ウサギ　よんわ four rabbits

*usagi gowa* ウサギ　ごわ five rabbits

*tori rokuwa* とり　ろくわ six birds

*tori nanawa* とリ　ななわ seven birds

*koumori hachiwa* コウモリ　はちわ eight bats

*koumori kyuuwa* コウモリ　きゅうわ nine bats

*koumori juuwa* コウモリ　じゅうわ ten bats

## Listen to track 19

冊 *(satsu)* counter for books

*hon issatsu* ほん　いっさつ one book

*hon nisatsu* ほん　にさつ two books

*hon sansatsu* ほん　さんさつ three books

*hon yonsatsu* ほん　よんさつ four books

*hon gosatsu* ほん　ごさつ five books

*hon rokusatsu* ほん　ろくさつ six books

*hon nanasatsu* ほん　ななさつ seven books

*hon hassatsu* ほん　はっさつ eight books

*hon kyuusatsu* ほん　きゅうさつ nine books

*hon jussatsu* ほん　じゅっさつ ten books

## Listen to track 20

台 *(dai)* counter for vehicles, furniture, electronics, large instruments, and whole cakes

*kuruma ichidai* くるま　いちだい one car

*torakku nidai* トラック　にだい two trucks

*hondana sandai* ほんだな　さんだい three bookshelves

*keeki yondai* ケーキ　よんだい four whole cakes

*baiku godai* バイク　ごだい five motorcycles

*piano rokudai* ピアノ　ろくだい six pianos

*doramu nanadai* ドラム　ななだい seven drum sets

*kurumaisu hachidai* くるまいす　はちだい eight wheelchairs

*kuruma kyuudai* くるま　きゅうだい nine cars

*kuruma juudai* くるま　じゅうだい ten cars

## *Listen to track 21*

### 分 *(fun/pun)* counter for minutes

*ippun* いっぷん 1 minute

*nifun* にふん 2 minutes

*sanpun* さんぷん 3 minutes

*yonpun* よんぷん 4 minutes

*gofun* ごふん 5 minutes

*roppun* ろっぷん 6 minutes

*nanafun* ななふん 7 minutes

*happun* はっぷん 8 minutes

*kyuufun* きゅうふん 9 minutes

*juppun* じゅっぷん 10 minutes

## *Listen to track 22*

### 年 *(nen)* years

*ichinen* いちねん 1 year

*ninen* にねん 2 years

*sannen* さんねん 3 years

*yonen* よねん 4 years

*gonen* ごねん 5 years

*rokunen* ろくねん 6 years

*nananen* ななねん 7 years

*hachinen* はちねん 8 years

*kyuunen* きゅうねん 9 years

*juunen* じゅうねん 10 years

## *Listen to track 23*

### 日 *(nichi/ka)* counter for days

Note that one is pronounced as (*tsuitachi* ついたち) for "the first of" when talking about the days of the month rather than the number of days.

*ichinichi* いちにち 1 day

*futsuka* ふつか 2 days

*mikka* みっか 3 days

*yokka* よっか 4 days

*itsuka* いつか 5 days

*muika* むいか 6 days

*nanoka* なのか 7 days

*youka* ようか 8 days

*kokonoka* ここのか 9 days

*tooka* とおか 10 days

## *Listen to track 24*

## 人 *(nin)* counter for people

There are some special readings for certain numbers as shown below.

*hitori* ひとり one person

*futari* ふたり two people

*sannin* さんにん three people

*yonin* よにん four people

*gonin* ごにん five people

*rokunin* ろくにん six people

*nananin* ななにん seven people

*hachinin* はちにん eight people

*kyuunin* きゅうにん nine people

*juunin* じゅうにん ten people

## *Listen to track 25*

## ケ月 *(kagetsu)* counter for months

*ikkagetsu* いっかけつ one month

*nikagetsu* にかげつ two months

*sankagetsu* さんかげつ three months

*yonkagetsu* よんかげつ four months

*gokagetsu* ごかげつ five months

*rokkagetsu* ろっかげつ six months

*nanakagetsu* ななかげつ seven months

*hakkagetsu* はっかげつ eight months

*kyuukagetsu* きゅうかげつ nine months

*jukkagetsu* じゅっかげつ ten months

## *Listen to track 26*

## 時 *(ji)* o'clock

*ichiji* いちじ 1 o'clock

*niji* にじ 2 o'clock

*sanji* さんじ 3 o'clock

*yoji* よじ 4 o'clock

*goji* ごじ 5 o'clock

*rokuji* ろくじ 6 o'clock

*shichiji* しちじ 7 o'clock

*hachiji* はちじ 8 o'clock

*kuji* くじ 9 o'clock

*juuji* じゅうじ 10 o'clock

*juuichiji* じゅういちじ 11 o'clock

*juuniji* じゅうにじ 12 o'clock

## *Listen to track 27*

### 時間　*(jikan)* counter for hours

*ichijikan* いちじかん 1 hour

*nijikan* にじかん 2 hours

*sanjikan* さんじかん 3 hours

*yojikan* よじかん 4 hours

*gojikan* ごじかん 5 hours

*rokujikan* ろくじかん 6 hours

*nanajikan* ななじかん 7 hours

*hachijikan* はちじかん 8 hours

*kujikan* くじかん 9 hours

*juujikan* じゅうじかん 10 hours

## *Listen to track 28*

### 回　*(kai)* counter for occurrences

*ikkai*　いっかい once

*nikai*　にかい twice

*sankai* さんかい three times

*yonkai* よんかい four times

*gokai*　ごかい five times

*rokkai* ろっかい six times

*nanakai*　ななかい seven times

*hakkai / hachikai* はっかい / はちかい
eight times

*kyuukai* きゅうかい nine times

*jukkai* じゅっかい ten times

## *Listen to track 29*

### 階　*(kai/gai)* counter for floors

*Ikkai*　いっかい first floor

*nikai*　にかい second floor

*sangai / sankai* さんがい・さんかい
third floor

*yonkai* よんかい fourth floor

*gokai*　ごかい fifth floor

*rokkai*　ろっかい sixth floor

*nanakai*　ななかい seventh floor

*hakkai / hachikai* はっかい・はちかい
eighth floor

*kyuukai* きゅうかい ninth floor

*jukkai* じゅっかい tenth floor

**_Listen to track 30_**

## 歳/才 *(sai)* counter for ages

*issai* いっさい 1 years old

*nisai* にさい 2 years old

*sansai* さんさい 3 years old

*yonsai* よんさい 4 years old

*gosai* ごさい 5 years old

*rokusai* ろくさい 6 years old

*nanasai* ななさい 7 years old

*hassai* はっさい eight years old

*kyuusai* きゅうさい nine years old

*jussai* じゅっさい ten years old

*for twenty years old, a special reading – *hatachi* はたち – is used.

# Making larger numbers: The teens, tens, combining tens and singles

If you know the numbers 1 to 10, you will be able to form numbers 11 to 99. To make 11, say ten-one (*juuichi*), 12 is ten-two (*juuni*), 13 is ten-three and so on. To make twenty, say two-ten (*nijuu*), 21 is two-ten-one (*nijuuni*), 22 is two-ten-two (*nijuuni*), and so on.

**_Listen to track 31_**

| Number | Kanji | On-reading | Kun-reading | Most commonly used reading |
|---|---|---|---|---|
| 11 | 十一 | *juuichi* | - | *juuichi* |
| 12 | 十二 | *juuni* | - | *juuni* |
| 13 | 十三 | *juusan* | - | *juusan* |
| 14 | 十四 | *juushi* | *juuyon* | *juushi* |
| 15 | 十五 | *juugo* | - | *juugo* |
| 16 | 十六 | *juuroku* | - | *juuroku* |
| 17 | 十七 | *juushichi* | *juunana* | *juunana* |
| 18 | 十八 | *juuhachi* | - | *juuhachi* |
| 19 | 十九 | *juukyuu/juuku* | - | *juukyuu/juuku* |
| 20 | 二十 | *nijuu* | *hata* | *nijuu* |
| 21 | 二十一 | *nijuuichi* | - | *nijuuichi* |
| 22 | 二十二 | *nijuuni* | - | *nijuuni* |
| 23 | 二十三 | *nijuusan* | - | *nijuusan* |
| 24 | 二十四 | *nijuushi* | - | *nijuushi* |

| 25 | 二十五 | nijuugo | - | nijuugo |
|----|--------|---------|---|---------|
| 26 | 二十六 | niijuuroku | - | niijuuroku |
| 27 | 二十七 | nijuushichi | nijuunana | nijuunana |
| 28 | 二十八 | nijuuhachi | - | nijuuhachi |
| 29 | 二十九 | nijuukyuu/nijuuku | - | nijuukyuu |
| 30 | 三十 | sanjuu | miso | sanjuu |
| 40 | 四十 | yonjuu | yoso | yonjuu |
| 50 | 五十 | gojuu | iso | gojuu |
| 60 | 六十 | rokujuu | muso | rokujuu |
| 70 | 七十 | shichijuu | nanaso | nanajuu |
| 80 | 八十 | hachijuu | yaso | hachijuu |
| 90 | 九十 | kyuujuu | kokonoso | kyuujuu |

## A little quiz

### Exercise 3

Write these *romaji* as numerals.

1. *sanjuu* _____
2. *juushichi* _____
3. *gojuu* _____

4. *nanajuuichi* _____
5. *rokujuuhachi* _____
6. *kyuujuugo* _____

### Answer key

Write these *romaji* as numerals.

1. *sanjuu* <u>30</u>
2. *juushichi* <u>17</u>
3. *gojuu* <u>50</u>

4. *nanajuuichi* <u>71</u>
5. *rokujuuhachi* <u>68</u>
6. *kyuujuugo* <u>95</u>

### Exercise 4

Write these numbers as *romaji*.

1. 25 _____
2. 92 _____
3. 30 _____

4. 40 _____
5. 68 _____
6. 11 _____

### Answer key

Write these numbers as *romaji*.

1. 25 <u>*niijuugo*</u>
2. 92 <u>*kyuujuuni*</u>
3. 30 <u>*sanjuu*</u>

4. 40 <u>*yonjuu*</u>
5. 68 <u>*rokujuuhachi*</u>
6. 11 <u>*juuichi*</u>

# Advanced numbers: the hundreds and thousands & putting all the numbers together

These numbers will come in handy when dealing with money in Japan as the bills are 1000 yen, 5,000 yen, and 10,000 yen. 100 yen coins and 500 yen coins are used.

### _Listen to track 32_

| Number | Kanji | On-reading | Kun-reading | Most commonly used reading |
|---|---|---|---|---|
| 100 | 百 | hyaku | momo | hyaku |
| 101 | 百一 | hyakuichi | - | hyakuichi |
| 150 | 百五十 | hyakugojuu | - | hyakugojuu |
| 191 | 百九十一 | hyakukyuujuuichi | - | hyakukyuujuuichi |
| 500 | 五百 | gohyaku | io | gohyaku |
| 800 | 八百 | happyaku | yao | happyaku |
| 1000 | 千 | sen | chi | sen |
| 1001 | 千一 | senichi | - | senichi |
| 1050 | 千五十 | sengojuu | - | sengojuu |
| 1200 | 千二百 | sennihyaku | - | sennihyaku |
| 1560 | 千五百六十 | sengohyakurokujuu | - | sengohyakurokujuu |
| 2000 | 二千 | nisen | - | nisen |
| 10,000 | 万 | man | yorozu | man |
| 100,000 | 百万 | hyakuman | - | hyakuman |
| 100,000,000 | 億 | oku | - | oku |
| 100,000,000,000 | 兆 | chou | - | chou |
| 10,000,000,000,000,000 | 京 | kei | - | kei |

## A little quiz

## Exercise 5

Write these *romaji* as numerals.

1. *ichiman* _____
2. *hyakuman* _____
3. *sen* _____

4. *hyaku* _____
5. *gohyaku* _____
6. *happyaku* _____

## Answer key

Write these *romaji* as numerals.

1. *ichiman* <u>10,000</u>
2. *hyakuman* <u>100,000</u>
3. *sen* <u>1,000</u>

4. *hyaku* <u>100</u>
5. *gohyaku* <u>500</u>
6. *happyaku* <u>800</u>

## Exercise 6

Write these numbers as words.

1. 250 _____
2. 920 _____
3. 30,000 _____

4. 500 _____
5. 100 _____
6. 4000 _____

## Answer key

Write these numbers as words.

1. 250 *nihyakugojuu*
2. 920 *kyuuhyakunijuu*
3. 30,000 *sanman*

4. 500 *gohyaku*
5. 100 *hyaku*
6. 4000 *yonsen*

# Basic math terminology

Many Japanese learners learn to count, but many of them miss out on learning the basic calculation words until they actually need to use them. Here are some math-related words that are useful to know.

### *Listen to track 33*

## Plus

たす *tasu*

1 + 2 = 3 (*ichi tasu ni wa san*)

## Minus

ひく  *hiku*

3 - 2 = 1 (*san hiku ni wa ichi*)

## Times

かける *kakeru*

4 x 2 = 8 (*yon kakeru ni wa hachi*)

## Divide

わる *waru*

6/2 = 3 (*roku waru ni wa san*)

## Equals

"Equals" is often said using the particle は (*wa*), but the English loanword イコール (*ikooru*) is also used.

## A little quiz

## Exercise 7

Write these math problems as words.

1.  2 + 5 = 8 _____
2.  10 - 3 = 7 _____
3.  4 x 8 = 32 _____
4.  4 / 2 = 2 _____

## Answer key

Write these math problems as words.

1.  2 + 5 = 8 *ni tasu go wa hachi*
2.  10 - 3 = 7 *juu hiku san wa nana*
3.  4 x 8 = 32 *yon kakeru hachi wa sanjuuni*
4.  4 / 2 = 2 *yon waru ni wa ni*

## Exercise 8

Write these math problems as numerals.

1.  *ichi tasu juu wa juuichi* _____
2.  *kyuu hiku yon wa go* _____
3.  *hachi kakeru san wa nijuuyon* _____
4.  *juu waru go wa ni* _____

## Answer key

Write these math problems as numerals.

1.  *ichi tasu juu wa juuichi* *1 + 10 = 11*
2.  *kyuu hiku yon wa go* *9 - 4 = 5*
3.  *hachi kakeru san wa nijuuyon* *8 x 3 = 24*
4.  *juu waru go wa ni* *10 / 5 = 2*

# Listening

## Listen to track 34

The verbs **arimasu** (base verb - **aru**, meaning "to be") and **motteimasu** (base verb - **motsu**, meaning "to have") can both be used to indicate possession.

The word **nani** (何) means "what," but **nan + counter (何 + counter)** means "**How many ~?**"

When you form a question you use the particle **ka** (か) at the end of the sentence.

*mo = also

*to = and

## Listen to track 35

Anna: *Riku-san, kaban ga omosou desu ne. nani wo motteimasu ka.*

アナ: りくさん、カバン が おもそう です ね。何 を もっていますか.

Anna: Riku, your bag looks heavy. What do you have?

Riku: *hon wo juusatsu motteimasu. pen gohon to sandoicchi sanko, to coora ippon mo arimasu.*

りく: ほん を 十冊 もっています。ペン 五本 と サンドイッチ 三個 と コーラ 一本 も あります。

Riku: I have ten books. I also have five pens, three sandwiches, and a bottle of Cola.)

Anna: *sugoi! ! takusan!*

アナ:すごい! たくさん!

Anna: Wow! So much!

Riku: *Anna-san wa doubutsu ga suki desu ne. petto wo katteimasu ka.*

りく: アナさん は どうぶつ が すき です ね。ペット を かっています か。

Riku: Anna, you like animals, don't you? Do you have any pets?

Anna: *inu sanbiki to hamusutaa ippiki, to neko gohiki wo katteimasu.*

アナ: イヌ 三匹 と ハムスター 一匹 と ネコ 五匹 を かっています。

Anna: I have three dogs, one hamster, and five cats.

Riku: *sugoi! takusan!*

りく: すごい! たくさん!

Riku: Wow! So many!

*The verb *kau (katteimasu)* means "to have" when talking about keeping animals.

### Listen to Track 35 and answer the following questions.

1. How many pens does Riku have? _____
2. How many books does Riku have? _____
3. How many cats does Anna have? _____
4. How many dogs does Anna have? _____
5. How many hamsters does Anna have? _____

## Answer key

### Listen to Track 35 and answer the following questions.

1. How many pens does Riku have? <u>Five pens</u>
2. How many books does Riku have? <u>Ten books</u>
3. How many cats does Anna have? <u>Five cats</u>
4. How many dogs does Anna have? <u>Three dogs</u>
5. How many hamsters does Anna have? <u>One hamster</u>

# Lesson activities

## Exercise 9

Write these numbers in romaji.

1. 100 _____
2. 800 _____
3. 10 _____
4. 50 _____
5. 80 _____
6. 1,000 _____
7. 8 _____
8. 1,400 _____
9. 379 _____
10. 12 _____

## Exercise 10

Write these words as numerals.

1. *san* _____
2. *hyakujuuhachi* _____
3. *yonjuu* _____
4. *nanajuuichi* _____
5. *senhappyaku* _____
6. *senkyuujuu* _____
7. *nihyakusanjuuroku* _____
8. *nanasengojuuichi* _____
9. *juuyon* _____
10. *kyuujuukyuu* _____

## Exercise 11

Write these in romaji using the correct number and counter.

1. 1 cat (*neko*) _____
2. 2 pens (*pen*) _____
3. 3 boxes (*hako*) _____
4. 4 birds (*tori*) _____
5. 5 years old _____

6. 6 times   _____

7. 7th floor   _____

8. 8 books (*hon*)   _____

9. 9 cars (*kuruma*)   _____

10. 10 hours   _____

## Exercise 12

Write the readings of these math problems in romaji.

1. 7 + 10 = 17   _____
2. 20 - 1 = 19   _____
3. 100 - 50 = 50   _____
4. 70 + 7 = 77   _____
5. 48 / 24 = 2   _____
6. 25 / 5 = 5   _____
7. 8 x 3 = 24   _____
8. 10 x 10 = 100   _____
9. 4 x 3 = 12   _____
10. 50 / 2 = 25   _____

## Exercise 13

Write the readings of these math problems in numerals.

1. *juu tasu hachi ha juuhachi*   _____
2. *ichi tasu ni wa san*   _____
3. *yon tasu roku wa juu*   _____
4. *roku kakeru roku wa sanjuuroku*   _____
5. *juuichi kakeru san wa sanjuusan*   _____
6. *hachi hiku ni wa roku*   _____
7. *juu hiku go wa go*   _____
8. *nana hiku ni wa go*   _____
9. *ni waru ni wa ichi*   _____
10. *kyuu waru san wa san*   _____

## Exercise 14

Write these numbers in kanji.

1. 100 _____
2. 800 _____
3. 10 _____
4. 50 _____
5. 80 _____
6. 1,000 _____
7. 8 _____
8. 1,400 _____
9. 379 _____
10. 12 _____

## Exercise 15

Write these with the number and counter in kanji and the word in hiragana or katakana.

1. 1 cat (*neko - katakana*) _____
2. 2 pens (*pen - katakana*) _____
3. 3 boxes (*hako - hiragana*) _____
4. 4 birds (*tori - hiragana*) _____
5. 5 years old _____
6. 6 times _____
7. 7th floor _____
8. 8 books (*hon - hiragana*) _____
9. 9 cars (*kuruma - hiragana*) _____
10. 10 hours _____

## Answer key

### Exercise 9

Write these numbers in romaji.

1. *100 hyaku*
2. *800 happyaku*
3. *10 juu*
4. *50 gojuu*
5. *80 hachijuu*

6. *1,000 sen*
7. *8 hachi*
8. *1,400 senyonhyaku*
9. *379 sanbyakunanajuugo*
10. *12 juuni*

### Exercise 10

Write these words as numerals.

1. *san 3*
2. *hyakujuuhachi 88*
3. *yonjuu 40*
4. *nanajuuichi 71*
5. *senhappyaku 1800*

6. *senkyuujuu 1090*
7. *nihyakusanjuuroku 236*
8. *nanasengojuuichi 7051*
9. *juuyon 14*
10. *kyuujuukyuu 99*

### Exercise 11

Write these in Japanese using the correct number and counter.

1. 1 cat *(neko) neko ippiki*
2. 2 pens *(pen) pen nihon*
3. 3 boxes *(hako) hako sanko*
4. 4 birds *(tori) tori yonwa*
5. 5 years old *gosai*

6. 6 times *rokkai*
7. 7th floor *nanakai*
8. 8 books *(hon) hon hassatsu*
9. 9 cars *(kuruma) kuruma kyuudai*
10. 10 hours *juujikan*

### Exercise 12

Write the readings of these math problems in romaji.

1. 7 + 10 = 17 *nana tasu juu wa juunana*
2. 20 - 1 = 19 *nijuu hiku ichi wa juukyuu*
3. 100 - 50 = 50 *hyaku hiku gojuu wa gojuu*
4. 70 + 7 = 77 *nanajuu tasu nana wa nanajuunana*
5. 48 / 24 = 2 *yonjuuhachi waru nijuuyon wa ni*
6. 25 / 5 = 5 *nijuugo waru go wa go*
7. 8 x 3 = 24 *hachi kakeru san wa nijuuyon*

8. 10 x 10 = 100 *juu kakeru juu wa hyaku*

9. 4 x 3 = 12 *yon kakeru san wa juuni*

10. 50 / 2 = 25 *gojuu waru ni wa nijuugo*

## Exercise 13

Write the readings of these math problems in numerals.

1. *juu tasu hachi wa juuhachi* 10 + 8 = 18

2. *ichi tasu ni wa san* 1 + 2 = 3

3. *yon tasu roku wa juu* 4 + 6 = 10

4. *roku kakeru roku wa sanjuuroku* 6 x 6 = 36

5. *juuichi kakeru san wa sanjuusan* 11 x 3 = 33

6. *hachi hiku ni wa roku* 8 - 2 = 6

7. *juu hiku go wa go* 10 - 5 = 5

8. *nana hiku ni wa go* 7 - 2 = 5

9. *ni waru ni wa ichi* 2/2 = 1

10. *kyuu waru san wa san* 9/3 = 3

## Exercise 14

Write these numbers in kanji.

1. 100 百
2. 800 八百
3. 10 十
4. 50 五十
5. 80 八十

6. 1,000 千
7. 8 八
8. 1,400 千四百
9. 379 三百七十九
10. 12 十二

## Exercise 15

Write these with the number and counter in kanji and the word in hiragana or katakana.

1. 1 cat (*neko - katakana*) ネコ　一匹
2. 2 pens (*pen - katakana*) ペン　二本
3. 3 boxes (*hako - hiragana*) はこ　三個
4. 4 birds (*tori - hiragana*) とり　四羽
5. 5 years old 五才/五歳
6. 6 times 六回

7. 7th floor 七階
8. 8 books (*hon - hiragana*) ほん　八冊
9. 9 cars (*kuruma - hiragana*) くるま　九台
10. 10 hours 十時間

In this lesson, you will learn:

- Culture tips relevant to first meetings
- How to introduce yourself
- How to introduce a friend
- How to ask someone's age
- How to say your age

## Culture corner

### Bowing

***Listen to track 36***

Bowing or *ojigi* (お辞儀) is perhaps the most well-known feature of Japanese etiquette. Bowing is used in cases such as greetings, introductions, showing appreciation, asking for a favor, congratulating, before and after a ceremony or meeting, and apologizing.

The custom of bowing is quite complex, as the length and depth of bow differs in each situation. The right way to bow in Japan is to bend from the waist with your back and neck straight, feet together, eyes looking downward, and arms straight by your sides. It is common for ladies to bow with their fingertips together or hands clasped in front of their thighs.

Bows of more than 45 degrees for around three seconds are used when apologizing for something serious or expressing extreme gratitude.

### Moving house

When you move into a new house in Japan, it is polite to introduce yourself to your neighbors and bring them a small gift such as sweets, snacks, a towel, etc.

Be sure to use both hands when you present the gift.

Listen to track 37

## Business cards - *meishi*

1. Keep your *meishi*, or business card, in a card case. If you do not have a card case yet, put the *meishi* in your wallet after you've received it. Putting it in your pocket is considered impolite.

2. Give and receive with two hands. (this etiquette rule is valid for handing over gifts and documents as well). The *meishi* should be facing toward the recipient. Hold the top edge with both hands when presenting the *meishi* to the recipient. When they offer their *meishi*, accept it with both hands. Avoid covering any words with your fingers if you can.

3. When you and your new acquaintance offer each other *meishi* at the same time, you can present your card with your right hand, while receiving their *meishi* with your left.

4. Read the *meishi* that you have received before you put it away. It is polite to show interest in what they do.

5. When exchanging *meishi* in a group, it is polite to give your *meishi* to the highest ranked person first. This means you should give your business card to the company president – the *shachou* – then the Vice President – the *fukushachou*.

6. Treat the *meishi* with respect. Don't throw them or write on them.

# Conversation

## Meeting someone for the first time

Here is an example dialogue of two people meeting for the first time.

Listen to track 38

**A: *hajimemashite, Yamada desu. yoroshiku onegai shimasu.*** \*

Nice to meet you. I am Yamada. Please get along with me.\*

**B: *hajimemashite. Suzuki desu. kochira koso, yoroshiku onegai shimasu.***

Nice to meet you. I am Suzuki. I hope you will get along with me too.

*Hajimemashite* translates as "Nice to meet you," but actually the word comes from the base verb *hajimeru*, meaning "to begin."

***Pro tip***: If you listen to Japanese people introducing themselves, you will notice the pitch of *hajimemashite* starts low, rises and then falls at the end.

\**Yoroshiku onegai shimasu* is a phrase that is difficult to translate into English, because it is used in many situations such as meeting someone for the first time, requesting something, an ending salutation on the phone or in an email, and starting an activity with someone.

It expresses the feeling that you hope you are able to interact well together or you hope someone will do something for you.

In formal situations, this can be lengthened to *douzo yoroshiku onegai shimasu,* or even shortened to *yoroshiku* in casual situations.

*kochira koso* is "**too**" in the English translation. However, it expresses that you want to return the same feeling to the person you are talking to.

Here is how to introduce an acquaintance to another acquaintance.

### Listen to track 39

**A: *kochira wa Sasaki-san desu.***

こちら は ささきさん です。

This is Mr/Mrs Sasaki.

**C: *hajimemashite. Sasaki desu. yoroshiku onegai shimasu.***

ささき です。よろしく おねがい します。

Nice to meet you. I am Mr/Mrs Sasaki. Please get along with me.

**B: *Sasaki-san, hajimemashite. Mori desu. kochira koso yoroshiku onegai shimasu.***

ささきさん、はじめまして。もり です。 こちら こそ よろしく おねがい します。

Nice to meet you, Mr/Mrs Sasaki. I am Mr/Mrs. Mori. I hope you will get along with me too.

Many Japanese introduce themselves with only their surname. In cases where they give their full name, they give their surname first and then their given name. Japanese people don't usually have middle names.

## About the honorific *-san*

The honorific *-san* follows after a name in Japanese, and is similar to the English "Mr" or "Mrs."

Notice how *-**san*** is not used when introducing yourself. Many Japanese accidentally introduce themselves with *-**san*** attached to their names, leading to some embarrassing first meetings. *-**san*** can be used after a surname or given name. For example: Yamada-san, Julie-san.

## Asking someone their age / saying your age

### *Listen to track 40*

The most polite way to ask someone's age is to say:

**oikutsu desu ka** (おいくつ　です　か。)

How old are you?

If you are on casual terms with a person, you may drop the "o" to become:

**ikutsu desu ka** (いくつ　です　か。)

How old are you?

**nansai desu ka** (なんさい　です　か。)

How old are you?

is usually used to ask about a third person's age or when talking to a child. A child may also ask you "**nansai desu ka.**"

## Listening

Listen to the conversation and answer the questions.

### *Listen to track 41*

Miyu: *Maria-san wa ikutsu desu ka*

Maria*: nansai ni miemasu ka.*

Miyu*: hatachi da to omoimasu.*

Maria: *niijuugosai desu. Miyu-san wa?*

Miyu: *sanjuusai desu. Maria-san no oniisan wa nansai desu ka.*

Maria: *nijuuhassai desu.*

### Grammar note:

*Name/pronoun + no + noun* indicates possession. For example *Maria-san no... =* "Maria's...."

*omoimasu (omou)* used with the particle *to* means "to think."

### Vocabulary:

*oniisan* = big brother

*miemasu (mieru)* = look/see

## A little quiz

1. How old is Maria?  _____
2. How old is Miyu?  _____
3. How old is Maria's older brother? _____

## Answer key

1. How old is Maria? *nijuugosai desu*
2. How old is Miyu? *sanjuusai desu*
3. How old is Maria's older brother? *nijuuhassai desu*

## Listening script

*Miyu: Maria-san wa ikutsu desu ka?*

みゆ: マリアさん　は　いくつ　です　か。

Miyu: How old are you, Maria?

*Maria: nansai ni miemasu ka?*

マリア: 何才　に　見えます　か。

Maria: How old do I look?

*Miyu: hatachi da to omoimasu.*

みゆ: 二十歳　だ　と　思います。

Miyu: I think you are 20 years old.

*Maria: niijuugosai desu. Miyu-san wa?*

マリア: 二十五才　です。みゆさん　は？

Maria: I am 25 years old. How about you?

*Miyu: sanjuusai desu. Maria-san no oniisan wa nansai desu ka?*

みゆ: 三十才　です。マリアさん　の　お兄さん　は　何才　です　か。

Miyu: I am 30 years old. How old is your big brother?

*Maria: nijuuhassai desu.*

マリア: 二十八才　です。

Maria: He's 28 years old.

# Speaking naturally

There are many ways to give your name in Japanese depending on the formality of the situation.

Compare these introductions:

### *Listen to track 42*

*Mori desu.* (common/polite)

もり　です。

I am Mr/Mrs.Mori.

*Mori Takeshi desu.* (common/polite)

もり　たけし　です。

I am Takeshi Mori.

*watashi no namae wa Mori Takeshi desu.* (full version of the above)

わたし　の　なまえ　は　もり　たけし　です。

My name is Takeshi Mori.

*Mori to iimasu.* (polite)

もり　と　いいます。

I am called Mr/Mrs.Mori.

*Mori Takeshi to moushimasu.* * (extremely polite)

もり　たけし　と　もうします。

I am called Takeshi Mori.

*When you use *moushimasu*, you should give your full name.

*ABC English School no Mori Takeshi to moushimasu* (business polite)

ABC イングリッシュ　スクール　の　もり　たけし　と　もうします

I am Takeshi Mori from ABC English School.

You may want your new Japanese friend to call you by a specific name. In which case you can introduce yourself like this.

**_Listen to track 43_**

**A:** *hajimemashite, Jones Kate desu. Kate to yonde kudasai. yoroshiku onegai shimasu.*

はじめまして。ジョーンズ　ケイト　です。ケイト　と　よんで　ください。よろしく　おねがい　します。

Nice to meet you. I am Kate Jones. You can call me Kate. Please get along with me.

**B:** *hajimemashite, Kate-san. Sakano Mizuki desu. Mizuki to yonde kudasai. kochira koso yoroshiku onegai shimasu.*

はじめまして。ケイトさん。さかの　みづき　です。みづき　と　よんで　ください。こちら　こそ　よろしく　おねがい　します。

Nice to meet you. I am Sakano Mizuki. I hope you will get along with me too.

We looked at many different ways to introduce yourself, but if you want to sound natural, you don't need to say "I" (*watashi* わたし). This is because the subject of the sentence is obvious from the context.

# Lesson activities

## Exercise 1

Write these phrases in *romaji*.

1. Nice to meet you. _____
2. I am Hannah Smith. _____
3. I am 19 years old. _____

## Exercise 2

Write these phrases in *hiragana* (you can review *hiragana* in lesson 1). Write any numbers or counters in *kanji* (you can review kanji and numbers in lesson 2).

1. My name is Sasaki Yuki. _____
2. I am 7 years old. _____
3. Please get along with me. _____

## Answer key

## Exercise 1

Write these phrases in romaji.

1. Nice to meet you. <u>*hajimemashite*</u>.
2. I am Hannah Smith. <u>*Sumisu Hana desu*</u>.
3. I am 19 years old. <u>*juukyuusai desu*</u>.

## Exercise 2

Write these phrases in *hiragana* (you can review *hiragana* in lesson 1). Write any numbers or counters in *kanji* (you can review kanji and numbers in lesson 2).

1. My name is Sasaki Yuki. <u>わたし　の　なまえ　は　ささき　ゆき　です。</u>
2. I am 7 years old. <u>七才　です。</u>
3. Please get along with me. <u>よろしく　おねがい します。</u>

# Lesson 4: Coming and going

Greetings are important and you will need them every day. We looked at greeting someone for the first time in the previous lesson, but now we will look at general greetings.

In this lesson, you will learn:

- How to greet people in different situations
- How to say "How are you?"
- How to speak naturally – the silent "u"
- Body vocabulary
- Vocabulary related to bed and bath

## Vocabulary

### Daily Greetings

### *Listen to track 44*

Hello/Good afternoon.

*konnichiwa*

こんにちは

Goodbye.

*sayounara*

さようなら

See you later.

*mata ne*

また　ね

See you tomorrow.

*mata ashita*

また　あした

Good morning.

*ohayou gozaimasu*

おはよう　ございます

Good evening.

*konbanwa*

こんばんは

Good night.

*oyasuminasai / oyasumi\**

おやすみなさい　/おやすみ

*informal

How are you?

*o-genki desu ka? / genki?\**

お元気ですか　/元気？

*informal

I am fine.

*genki desu / genki**

元気です。/ 元気

*informal

Excuse me. / I'm sorry.

*sumimasen.*

すみません

I'm sorry.

*gomen nasai. / gomen.**

ごめん　なさい　/ ごめん

*informal

No problem.*

*iie*

いいえ

*after someone apologizes

Thank you. / Thanks.

*arigatou gozaimasu.*

ありがとう　ございます　/ ありがとう

You're welcome

*douitashimashite*

どういたしまして

A phrase said before eating

*itadakimasu.*

いただきます

A phrase said after eating

*gochisousama. (deshita)*

ごちそうさま　（でした）

Note that the "wa" in *konnichiwa* and *konbanwa* are written using the hiragana "*ha*":
こんにちは，　こんばんは

## Dialogue

### Listen to track 45

*Mitsuki: \*don\* sumimasen!*

みつき: ＊ドン＊ すみません！

Mitsuki: \*bump\* Sorry!

*Takuya: iie. daijoubu?*

たくや: いいえ。だいじょうぶ？

Takuya: No worries. Are you okay?

*Mitsuki: hai, daijoubu. ohayou. genki?*

みつき：はい、だいじょうぶ。おはよう。げんき？

Mitsuki: Yes, I'm alright. Good morning. How's it going?

*Takuya: ohayou. genki da yo. Mitsuki-chan wa?*

たくや：おはよう。げんき　だ　よ。みつきちゃん　は？

Takuya: Good morning. I'm good. How about you?

*Mitsuki: un, genki. demo, isoideiru n da. sansuu no jugyou ga juuji ni hajimaru n da.*

みつき：うん、元気。でも、いそいでいる　ん　だ。さんすう　の　じゅぎょう
が　十時　に　はじまる　ん　だ。

Mitsuki: Yeah, I'm good. But, I'm in a rush. Math class starts at 10 o'clock.

*Takuya: aa, ato sanpun. isoide! mata ne.*

たくや：あぁ、あと　三分。いそいで！また　ね。

Takuya: Oh, you only have 3 minutes left. You better hurry! See you later.

*Mitsuki: mata ne.*

みつき：また　ね。

Mitsuki: See you.

**Grammar note:**

*n desu / n da* is used when giving new information.

**Vocabulary:**

*hai* はい　yes

*un* うん　yes (informal)

*daijoubu* 大丈夫　okay (use rising intonation to make it a question)

*daijoubu desu ka* 大丈夫　です　か　Are you okay? (polite)

*sansuu* 算数　mathematics

*jugyou* 授業　class

*isoideiru* (base verb - *isogu*) 急いでいる　hurrying (informal)

*isoide* (base verb - *isogu*) 急いで　hurry up

da だ   the informal form of *desu* - to be

ato 後   after/leftover/later

## Dialogue

### *Listen to track 46*

*okaasan: sorosoro neru jikan yo.*

お母さん: そろそろ　ねる　　じかん　よ。

Mother: It's time for bed soon.

*Mitsuki: hai.*

みつき: はい。

Mitsuki: Okay.

*okaasan: shukudai owatta?*

お母さん: しゅくだい　おわった？

Mother: Did you finish your homework?

*Mitsuki: hai, mama.*

みつき: はい、ママ。

Mitsuki: Yes, mom.

*okaasan: hai, gyuunyuu douzo. oyasumi.*

お母さん: はい、ぎゅうにゅう　どうぞ。おやすみ。

Mother: Here, have some milk. Good night.

*Mitsuki: oyasumi.*

みつき: おやすみ

Mitsuki: Good night.

## Vocabulary:

*okaasan* お母さん   mother

*neru* 寝る      sleep

*sorosoro* そろそろ   soon

*jikan* - 時間   time

*shukudai* 宿題   homework

*hai douzo* はい　どうぞ   here you are (when giving something)

*gyuunyuu* 牛乳   milk

# Listening

Listen to this dialogue and answer the questions.

## *Listen to track 47*

**Vocabulary:**

*maamaa* まあまあ   not bad

*resutoran* レストラン   restaurant

*ikimasen ka* 行きませんか   Would you like to go to…?

*ii desu ne* いい　です　ね   That sounds good. (used to accept an invitation)

*konya* 今夜   tonight

*deeto* デート   date

*kekkou desu* 結構　です   No, thank you. (used to politely refuse)

1.  Is it morning, afternoon, or evening?  _____
2.  What time will Suzuki-san go to the restaurant?  _____
3.  Does Sasaki-san want to go to the restaurant?  _____

## *Listen to track 48*
### The body 体　*karada*

| English | Romaji | Kanji |
|---|---|---|
| head | *atama* | 頭 |
| shoulders | *kata* | 肩 |
| knees | *hiza* | 膝 |
| toes | *ashiyubi* | 足指 |
| eyes | *me* | 目 |
| ears | *mimi* | 耳 |
| mouth | *kuchi* | 口 |
| nose | *hana* | 鼻 |
| hair | *kami* | 髪 |
| nails | *tsume* | 爪 |

| face | *kao* | 顔 |
|------|-------|-----|
| arm | *ude* | 腕 |
| leg | *ashi* | 脚 |
| foot | *ashi* (same as leg, but uses a different kanji) | 足 |

## *Listen to track 49*

## Bed and bath ベッド　と　お風呂　*beddo to ofuro*

| English | Romaji | Kanji/Kana |
|---------|--------|------------|
| bed | *beddo* | ベッド |
| futon | *futon* | 布団 |
| pillow | *makura* | 枕 |
| duvet | *kakebuton* | 掛け布団 |
| futon mat | *shikibuton* | 敷布団 |
| pajamas | *pajama* | パジャマ |
| bath | *ofuro* | お風呂 |
| shower | *shawaa* | シャワー |
| soap | *sekken* | 石鹸 |
| body soap | *bodiisoopu* | ボディーソープ |
| sponge | *suponji* | スポンジ |
| toothbrush | *haburashi* | 歯ブラシ |
| toothpaste | *hamigakiko* | 歯磨き粉 |
| face wash | *senganryou* | 洗顔料 |
| moisturizing cream | *hoshitsukuriimu* | 保湿クリーム |

# Culture clip

## Leaving and returning home

There are some set phrases used when leaving home and returning home.

They are:

## *Listen to track 50*

*ittekimasu* いってきます - I'm going out. (said when leaving home)

*itterasshai* いってらっしゃい - Take care. (said to the person leaving home)

*tadaima* ただいま - I'm home. (said when returning home)

*okaeri* おかえり - Welcome back. (said to the person who came back home)

Let's look at an example.

**Vocabulary:**

*benkyou* 勉強 studies

*ganbatte* 頑張って (base verb - *ganbaru*) do your best

*otousan* お父さん　father

*tesuto* テスト　test

*kekka* 結果　result

*misete* 見せて (base verb - *miseru* 見せる)　to show

### *Listen to track 51*

*Takuya: okaasan, ittekimasu.*

たくや: おかあさん、行ってきます。

Takuya: I'm going now, mom.

*okaasan: itterasshai. benkyou ganbatte.*

お母さん: いってらっしゃい。べんきょう　がんばって。

Mother: Come back safely. Study hard.

*Takuya: hai.*

たくや: はい。

Takuya: Okay.

*Takuya: tadaima.*

たくや: ただいま。

Takuya: I'm back.

*otousan: okaeri. tesuto no kekka wo misete.*

お父さん: おかえり。テスト の 結果 を 見せて。

Father: Welcome back. Show me your test results.

*Takuya: aa….hai.*

たくや: あぁ。。。はい。

Takuya: Ah…okay.

## *Otsukaresama desu / Otsukaresama deshita*

This phrase is used amongst people working together. It doesn't have a set translation as it is used in various situations, but it is derived from the word *tsukareru* – to be tired. **otsukaresama deshita** is said before leaving the office and could be translated as "Thanks for your hard work," along with **saki ni shitsurei shimasu** which literally means, "Sorry, I am leaving before you."

*desu* is the present simple form of the verb *to be* when being used as a polite sentence ender.

*deshita* is the past simple form of the same word.

Take a look at this conversation:

## Dialogue

### Listen to track 52

*Sasaki: otsukaresama desu. miitingu wa dou deshita?*

ささき：おつかれさま　です。ミーティング　は　どう　でした？

Sasaki: You must be tired. How was the meeting?

*Minami: umaku itta to omoimasu. ashita no pawaapointo wa owarimashita ka?*

みなみ：うまく　いった　と　おもいます。あした　の　パワーポイント　は　おわりました　か？

Minami: I think it went well. Did you finish the PowerPoint for tomorrow?

*Sasaki: sumimasen, mada desu.*

ささき：すみません。まだです。

Sasaki: Sorry. Not yet.

*Minami: yoroshiku onegaishimasu.*

みなみ：よろしく　おねがい　します。

Minami: Please do so.

*Nanase: Sasaki-san, Minami san. saki ni shitsurei shimasu. otsukaresama deshita.*

ななせ：ささきさん、みなみさん、さき　に　しつれい　します。おつかれさま　でした。

Nanase: Sasaki-san, Minami-san. I'm going home now. Thanks for your hard work.

*Sasaki/Minami: otsukaresama.*

ささき/みなみ: おつかれさま.

*Sasaki/Minami: Thanks for your hard work.*

## Shitsurei shimasu

*shitsurei* literally means "rude."

*shimasu* is the polite form of *suru* meaning "to do."

The phrase *shitsurei shimasu* has a variety of uses:

1. Said before entering someone's house or office.
2. Said before ending a phone call.
3. Said to apologize.

Take a look at this example dialogue:

## Listen to track 53

*Risa: shitsurei shimasu.*

リサ: しつれい　します。

Lisa: Excuse me.

*sensei: Risa-chan, douzo haitte kudasai. dou shimashita ka.*

先生: リサちゃん、どうぞ　入って　ください。どう　しました　か。

Teacher: Lisa-chan, please come in. What's the matter?

*Risa: shukudai ga wakarimasen.*

リサ: しゅくだい が　わかりません。

Lisa: I don't understand my homework.

## Ojama shimasu / Ojama shimashita

*ojama shimasu* is derived from the word *jama* meaning "to disturb" or "to be in the way." It is used similarly to *shitsurei shimasu*, but said when entering someone's house.

*ojama shimashita* is in the past simple form and is said when you leave someone's house.

### Listen to track 54

*Risa: ojama shimasu.*

リサ: おじゃま　します。

Lisa: Sorry to disturb you.

*Mitsuki: haitte! haitte! surippa douzo.*

みつき: はいって！はいって！スリッパ　どうぞ。

Mitsuki: Come in! Come in! Here are some slippers.

*Risa: arigatou.*

リサ: ありがとう。

Lisa: Thanks.

### Itadakimasu / Gochisousama deshita

*itadakimasu* is an expression said before eating. It is derived from the word *itadaku* meaning "to receive." It's often translated as "*Let's eat.*"

*gochisousama deshita* is said after finishing a meal and can be translated to "*Thank you for the meal.*" It is often shortened to *gochisousama*.

Take a look at this sample dialogue:

### Listen to track 55

*Risa / Mitsuki: itadakimasu.*

リサ/みつき: いただきます

Risa/Mitsuki: Let's eat.

*Risa: oishii.*

リサ: おいしい

Risa: It's tasty.

*Mitsuki: arigatou. nihon no tabemono wa suki?*

みつき: ありがとう。にほん　の　たべもの　は　すき？

Mitsuki: Thanks. Do you like Japanese food?

*Risa: un, suki. yakitori ga ichiban suki nan da.*

リサ：うん、すき。やきとり　が　いちばん　すき　なん　だ。

Lisa: Yeah, I like it. I like yakitori best.

*Mitsuki: watashi wa sushi ga ichiban suki nan da.*

みつき：わたし　は　すし　が　いちばん　すき　なん　だ。

Mitsuki: I like sushi best.

## Vocabulary:

*oishii* おいしい　delicious

*nihon* 日本　Japan

*nihon no* にほん　の　Japanese (things, not people)

*tabemono* 食べ物　food

*suki* 好き　like

*ichiban* 一番　the best / number one

## Grammar note:

*nan da / nan desu* is the same as *n da / n desu* but comes after a word that is not a verb, whereas *n da* and *n desu* come after a verb. It is used when giving new information.

# Speaking naturally

## The silent "U" sound

When you see words with "u" at the end or in the middle such as *desu*, *kutsu*, and *shimasu*, you may be tempted to say it as you see it, but if you listen to native speakers, you will notice this sound is often silent.

It isn't wrong to pronounce it per se, but you will sound cute or childish.

Some common examples of words where the *u* sound seems to disappear:

### *Listen to track 56*

*desu* です to be (polite)

*sugoi* 凄い great

*subarashii* すばらしい wonderful

*bikkurishita* びっくりした I was surprised.

*kutsu* 靴 shoes

# Lesson activities

## Exercise 1

Answer the questions using romaji.

1. You see a neighbor in the morning. Greet them.

   _____

2. You see your friend in the afternoon. Greet them.

   _____

3. Say "see you tomorrow" to your friend.

   _____

4. Say "good night" to a family member.

   _____

5. Say "goodbye" to your teacher.

   _____

6. Ask your friend how they are.

   _____

7. Your co-worker looks sick. Ask them if they are okay.

   _____

8. You stood on someones' foot. Apologize to them.

   _____

9. Your coworker gave you a souvenir from their holiday. Thank them.

   _____

10. You are about to have a meal with a friend. What do you say?

    _____

## Exercise 2

Write these words in kana or kanji.

1. *konnichiwa* _____
2. *konbanwa* _____
3. *oyasumi nasai* _____
4. *arigatou gozaimasu* _____
5. *gochisousama deshita* _____
6. *ojama shimasu* _____
7. *itadakimasu* _____
8. *ohayou gozaimasu* _____

9. *oishii* _____

10. *suki* _____

11. *benkyou* _____

12. *ichiban* _____

13. *nihon* _____

14. *tabemono* _____

15. *sumimasen* _____

## Answer key

### Exercise 1

Answer the questions using romaji.

1. You see a neighbor in the morning. Greet them. *ohayou gozaimasu*
2. You see your friend in the afternoon.Greet them. *konnichiwa*
3. Say "see you tomorrow" to your friend. *mata ashita*
4. Say "good night" to a family member. *oyasumi*
5. Say "goodbye" to your teacher. *sayonara*
6. Ask your friend how they are. *genki?*
7. Your co-worker looks sick. Ask them if they are okay. *daijoubu desu ka*
8. You stood on someones' foot. Apologize to them. *Sumimasen*
9. Your coworker gave you a souvenir from their holiday. Thank them. *arigatou gozaimasu*
10. You are about to have a meal with a friend. What do you say? *itadakimasu*

### Exercise 2

Write these words in kana or kanji.

1. *konnichiwa* こんにちは
2. *konbanwa* こんばんは
3. *oyasumi nasai* おやすみ　なさい
4. *arigatou gozaimasu* ありがとう　ございます
5. *gochisousama deshita* ごちそうさま　でした
6. *ojama shimasu* お邪魔　します　/ おじゃま　します
7. *itadakimasu* いただきます
8. *ohayou gozaimasu* おはよう　ございます
9. *oishii* おいしい

10. *suki* すき

11. *benkyou* 勉強　／べんきょう

12. *ichiban* 一番　／いちばん

13. *nihon* 日本　／にほん

14. *tabemono* 食べ物　／たべもの

15. *sumimasen* すみません

## Listening script

*Yamada: Suzuki-san, konbanwa.*

やまだ: すずきさん、こんばんは。

Yamada: Mr Suzuki, good evening.


*Suzuki: Mr Yamada, konbanwa. o-genki desu ka.*

すずき: やまださん、こんばんは。お元気ですか。

Suzuki: Mr. Yamada, good evening. How are you?


*Yamada: maamaa desu. Suzuki-san wa?*

やまだ: まあまあです。すずきさんは？

Yamada: I am not bad. How about you?


*Suzuki: genki desu. gogo rokuji ni resutoran ni ikimasen ka?*

すずき: げんきです。ごご　六時　に　レストラン　に　いきません　か。

Suzuki: I am fine. Would you like to go to a restaurant at 6pm?


*Yamada: ii desu ne.*

やまだ: いい　です　ね。

Yamada: Yes, that sounds good.


*Suzuki: Ah, Sasaki-san wa dou desu ka. issho ni resutoran ni ikimasen ka.*

すずき: あぁ、ささきさん　は　どう　です　か。いっしょに　レストラン　に　いきません　か。

Suzuki: Ah, Sasaki-san, how about you? Would you like to go with us to the restaurant?

*Sasaki: konya, deeto ga aru node, kekkou desu.*

ささき: こんや、デート が ある ので、けっこう　です。

Sasaki: I have a date tonight, so no thank you.

## Listening answers

1. Is it morning, afternoon or evening? <u>Evening</u>
2. What time will Suzuki-san go to the restaurant? <u>6pm</u>
3. Does Sasaki-san want to go to the restaurant? <u>No</u>

# Lesson 5: I am a student

In this lesson, you will learn:

- How to make sentences using *desu*
- How to say "There is / there are / I have" using *aru*
- The difference between *aru* and *iru*
- How to make plurals
- How to change statements into questions
- Honorifics

## Grammar

### Creating simple sentences

### A *wa* B *desu*

We have seen ***desu* (to be)** in dialogues in previous lessons.

***Da*** is the informal form of ***desu***.

Now we will try to form sentences using *desu*.

Look at the vocabulary below and sample sentences.

### *Listen to track 57*

私 は 七瀬 三月 です。

*watashi wa Nanase Mitsuki desu.*

I am Mitsuki Nanase.

ささきさん は 日本人 です。

*Sasaki-san wa nihonjin desu.*

Miss Sasaki is Japanese.

私 は アメリカ人 です。

*watashi wa amerikajin desu.*

I am American.

私 は 大学生 です。

*watashi wa daigakusei desu.*

I am a university student.

私 の 専攻 は 日本語 です。

*watashi no senkou wa nihongo desu.*

My major is Japanese.

私 は 会社員 です。

*watashi wa kaishain desu.*

I am an office worker.

## Vocabulary:

*nihonjin* 日本人　Japanese person

*amerikajin* アメリカ人　American person

*daigaku* 大学　university

*daigakusei* 大学生 university student

*senkou* 専攻　major

## Dialogue

### *Listen to track 58*

*Risa: konnichiwa. nihonjin desu ka.*

リサ: こんにちは。日本人　です　か。

Lisa: Hello. Are you Japanese?

*Takuya: hai, nihonjin desu. amerikajin desu ka.*

たくや: はい、日本人　です。アメリカ人　です　か。

Takuya: Yes, I am Japanese. Are you American?

*Risa: iie, igirisujin desu.*

リサ : いいえ、イギリス人　です。

Lisa: No, I am British.

*Takuya: sou desu ka. sensei desu ka.*

たくや: そう　です　か。先生　です　か。

Takuya: Really? Are you a teacher?

*Risa: chigaimasu,\* daigakusei desu.*

リサ: 違います。大学生　です。

Lisa: No, I am a university student.

*Takuya: senkou wa nihongo desu ka.*

たくや: せんこう　は　日本語　です　か。

Takuya: Is your major Japanese?

*Risa: sou desu.*

リサ:そうです。

Lisa: That's right.

*\*chigaimasu*　違います (base verb – *chigau*　違う) literally means "that is wrong."

# Listening

Listen to the dialogue and answer the questions.

### Listen to track 59

1. What nationality is Maria? _____
2. What is Maria's major? _____
3. What is Takuya's major? _____
4. What does Takuya's father do? _____
5. What does Takuya's mother do? _____

## There is / there are

## To have

### Listen to track 60

### Y ga arimasu / Y ga aru (informal)

The verb **aru** is a base verb meaning "to be" and is used to say that **something is there** or that you **have something**.

Note: This is used with non-living things.

***X ga imasu / Y ga iru*** (informal)

The verb ***iru*** is a base verb meaning "to be" and is used to say that **someone is there.**

Note: This is used with people and other living things.

## There isn't / there aren't

## Don't have

### *Listen to track 61*

***Y ga arimasen / Y ga nai*** (informal)

By changing -***masu*** to -***masen*** this verb can be made into the negative form.

***nai*** is the informal negative form of ***aru***, and ***inai*** is the informal negative form of ***iru***.

## Examples:

### *Listen to track 62*

*(watashi wa) kuruma ga arimasu.*

「私　は」車　が　あります。

I have a car.

*(watashi wa) geemuki ga nai.*

「私　は」ゲーム機　が　ない。

I don't have a game console.

*(watashi wa) toranpetto ga aru.*

「私　は」トランペット　が　ある。

I have a trumpet.

*(watashi wa) doramu ga arimasen.*

「私　は」ドラム　が　ありません。

I don't have any drums.

*Sasaki-san wa nooto pasokon ga arimasu.*

佐々木さん　は　ノートパソコン　が　あります。

Mr. Sasaki has a laptop computer.

*Sasaki-san wa taburetto ga arimasen.*

佐々木さん　は　タブレット　が　ありません。

Mr. Sasaki doesn't have a tablet.

*Mitsuki-san wa ningyou ga arimasu.*

三月さん　は　人形　が　あります。

Mitsuki has a doll.

*Mitsuki-san wa soccer ball ga arimasen.*

三月さん　は　サッカー　ボール　が　ありません。

Mitsuki doesn't have a soccer ball.

*(watashi wa) neko ga imasu.*

「私　は」猫　が　います。

I have a cat.

*Takuya-san wa inuwo katteimasen.*

たくやさん　は　犬　を飼っていません。

Takuya doesn't have a dog.

*jitensha ga aru.*

自転車　が　ある。

There is a bicycle.

*enpitsu ga arimasu.*

えんぴつ　が　あります。

There is a pencil. / I have a pencil.

*biru ga takusan aru.*

ビル　が　たくさん　ある。

There are many buildings.

*hana ga arimasu.*

花　が　あります。

There are flowers.

*usagi ga iru.*

ウサギ　が　いる

There are rabbits.

*kitsune ga imasu.*

キツネ　が　います。

There are foxes.

*hitsuji ga imasen.*

羊　が　いません

There are no sheep.

*ushi ga inai.*

牛　が　いない。

There are no cows.

## Vocabulary:

*enpitsu* えんぴつ　pencil

*kitsune* キツネ　fox

*usagi* ウサギ　rabbit

*hitsuji* 羊 sheep

ushi 牛　cow

*hana* 花　flower

*biru* ビル　building

*takusan* たくさん　many/a lot

*jitensha* 自転車　bicycle

*doramu* ドラム　drums

*toranpetto* トランペット　trumpet

## Dialogue

### Listen to track 63

*Mitsuki: nannin kazoku desu ka.*

みつき：何人　かぞく　です　か。

*Mitsuki: How many people are there in your family?*

Risa:    gonin kazoku desu. okaasan to otousan to oniisan to otouto ga imasu.

リサ: 五人　かぞく　です。お母さん　と　お父さん　と　お兄さん　と　弟　が　います。

*Lisa: There are five people in my family. I have a mother, father, big brother, and a little brother.*

*Mitsuki: watashi wa otousan to okaasan to imouto futari to oneesan ga imasu. rokunin kazoku desu.*

みつき: 私　は　お父さん　と　お母さん　と　妹　二人　と　お姉さん　が　います。六人　かぞく　です。

*Mitsuki: I have a father, mother, two little sisters, and a big sister. There are six people in my family.*

*Risa: Mitsuki-san no ryoushin wa kuruma wo motte imasu ka.*

リサ: みつきさん　の　りょうしん　は　くるま　を　もっていますか。

*Lisa: Mitsuki, do your parents have a car?*

*Mitsuki: hai, arimasu. kuruma ga nidai arimasu.*

みつき: はい、あります。くるま　が　二台　　あります。

*Mitsuki: Yes, they have. They have two cars.*

*Risa: ii desu ne.*

リサ: いい　です　ね。

*Lisa: That's nice.*

**Vocabulary:**

*otouto* 弟　little brother

*oniisan* お兄さん　big brother

*imouto* 妹 little sister

*oneesan* お姉さん　big sister

*ryoushin* 両親　parents

*ii desu ne* いいですね　That's nice/good.

# Listening

Listen to the dialogue and answer the questions.

### Listen to track 64

1. How many people are in Takuya's family?  _____
2. Does Takuya have a little sister?  _____
3. How many people are in Jack's family?  _____
4. Does Jack have a little brother?  _____
5. Does Jack's father have a car?  _____

## Plurals

Plurals are often not expressed as frequently as they are in English.

## Examples:

### Listen to track 65

There is a tree.

木　が　あります。

*ki ga arimasu.*

There are trees.

木　が　あります。

*ki ga arimasu.*

However, the use of the word *tachi* 達   can be used to express plural when talking about people.

## Examples:

### Listen to track 66

*kodomo-tachi*

子供達

*kids*

*sensei-tachi*

先生達

*teachers*

*gakusei-tachi*

学生達

*students*

*anata-tachi*

あなた達

you (plural)

*nanase-san-tachi*

七瀬さん達

Mr/Mrs.Nanase and the others

## Statements and questions

### Turning statements into questions using *ka*

Putting **ka** at the end of a statement changes it into a question.

Compare the statements below.

### *Listen to track 67*

*kaishain desu.*

会社員　です。

I am an office worker.

*kaishain desu ka.*

会社員　です　か。

Are you an office worker?

*hatachi desu.*

二十歳　です。

I am 20 years old.

*hatachi desu ka.*

二十歳　です　か。

Are you 20 years old?

*watashi no okaasan wa isha desu.*

私　の　お母さん　は　医者　です。

My mother is a doctor.

*okaasan wa isha desu ka.*

お母さん　は　医者　です　か。

Is your mother a doctor?

*sakana ga suki desu.*

魚　が　好き　です。

I like fish.

*sakana wa suki desu ka.*

魚　は　好き　です　か。

Do you like fish?

*watashi no suki na kamoku wa kagaku desu.*

私　の　好き　な　科目　は　科学　です。

My favorite subject is science.

*suki na kamoku wa kagaku desu ka.*

好き　な　科目　は　科学　です　か。

Is your favorite subject science.

*niku wo tabemasu.*

肉　を　食べます。

I eat meat.

*niku wo tabemasu ka.*

肉 を 食べます か。

Do you eat meat?

*Yamada desu.*

やまだ です。

I am Mr.Yamada.

*Yamada-san desu ka.*

やまださん です か。

Are you Mr.Yamada?

*tenisu wo shimasu.*

テニス を します。

I play tennis.

*tenisu wo shimasu ka.*

テニス を します か。

Do you play tennis?

*yakkyuu wo suru no ga suki desu.*

野球 を する の が 好き で
す。

I like to play baseball.

## Dialogue

*Jyakku: Takuya-san no suki na kamoku wa nan desu ka.*

ジャック: たくやさん の 好き な 科目 は 何 です か。

Jack: Takuya, what is your favorite subject?

*yakkyuu wo suru no ga suki desu ka.*

野球 を する の が 好き です
か。

Do you like to play baseball?

*hon wo yomu no ga suki desu.*

本 を 読む の が 好き です。

I like to read books.

*hon wo yomu no ga suki desu ka.*

本 を 読む の が 好き です
か。

Do you like to read books?

*terebi wo miru no ga suki desu.*

テレビ を 見る の が 好き で
す。

I like to watch TV.

*terebi wo miru no ga suki desu ka.*

テレビ を 見る の が 好き で
す か。

Do you like to watch TV?

*Takuya: watashi no suki na kamoku wa rekishi desu.*

たくや: 私　の　好き　な　科目　は　歴史　です。

Takuya: My favorite subject is history.

*Jyakku: shuumatsu ni nani wo suru no ga suki desu ka.*

ジャック: 週末　に　何　を　する　のが　好き　です　か。

Jack: What do you like to do on the weekend?

*Takuya: basukettobooru wo suru no ga suki desu. Jyakku-san wa niku ga suki desu ka.*

たくや: バスケットボール　を　する　の　が　好き　です。ジャックさん　は　肉　が　好き　です　か。

Takuya: I like to play basketball. Jack, do you like meat?

*Jyakku: hai, daisuki desu.*

ジャック: はい、大好き　です。

Jack: Yes, I love it.

*Takuya: yakiniku no resutoran ni ikimasen ka.*

たくや: 焼肉　の　レストラン　に　行きません　か。

Takuya: Do you want to go to a yakiniku restaurant?

*Jyakku: ii desu ne.*

ジャック: いい　です　ね。

Jack: That sounds good.

**Vocabulary:**

*kamoku* 科目 subject

*rekishi* 歴史 history

*basukettobooru* バスケットボール basketball

*niku* 肉 meat

*suki* 好き　like

*daisuki* 大好き　love

*yakiniku* 焼肉 yakiniku

*iku* 行く　go

# Vocabulary

## *Listen to track 70*

## University majors 専攻　*senkou*

| English | Romaji | Kanji/Kana |
|---|---|---|
| Japanese | *nihongo* | 日本語 |
| English | *eigo* | 英語 |
| Chinese | *chuugokugo* | 中国語 |
| Korean | *kankokugo* | 韓国語 |
| German | *doitsugo* | ドイツ語 |
| French | *furansugo* | フランス語 |
| Spanish | *supeingo* | スペイン語 |
| Arabic | *arabiago* | アラビア語 |
| Business | *bijinesu* | ビジネス |
| Art | *bijutsu* | 美術 |
| Medicine | *igaku* | 医学 |
| Psychology | *shinrigaku* | 心理学 |
| Philosophy | *tetsugaku* | 哲学 |
| History | *rekishi* | 歴史 |
| Religious Education | *shuukyou* | 宗教 |
| Politics | *seiji* | 政治 |
| Accountancy | *kaikeigaku* | 会計学 |
| Economics | *keizai* | 経済 |
| Sports | *supootsu* | スポーツ |
| Education | *kyouiku* | 教育 |
| Science | *kagaku* | 科学 |
| Music | *ongaku* | 音楽 |
| Mathematics | *sansuu* | 算数 |
| Architecture | *kenchikugaku* | 建築学 |
| Agriculture | *nougaku* | 農学 |
| Sociology | *shakaigaku* | 社会学 |
| Dentistry | *shikagaku* | 歯科学 |
| Nursing | *kangogaku* | 看護学 |
| Engineering | *kougaku* | 工学 |

| Astronomy | *tenmongaku* | 天文学 |
| Law | *hougaku* | 法学 |
| I.T. | *jouhougijutsu / aitii* | 情報技術　／アイティー |

## *Listen to track 71*

## Occupations 仕事 *shigoto*

| English | Romaji | Kanji/Kana |
|---|---|---|
| teacher | *sensei / kyoushi* | 先生　／教師 |
| doctor | *isha* | 医者 |
| lawyer | *bengoshi* | 弁護士 |
| musician | *ongakuka / musician* | 音楽家 |
| police officer | *keisatsukan* | 警察官 |
| firefighter | *shouboushi* | 消防士 |
| office worker | *kaishain* | 会社員 |
| game developer | *geemu kaihatsusha* | ゲーム　開発者 |
| engineer | *gijutsusha / enjinia* | 技術者　／エンジニア |
| computer engineer | *konpyuutaa enjinia / konpyuutaa gijutsusha* | コンピューターエンジニア　／コンピューター技術者 |
| sales assistant | *tenin* | 店員 |
| nurse | *kangoshi* | 看護師 |
| bus driver | *basu untenshu* | バス運転手 |
| taxi driver | *takushii untenshu* | タクシー運転手 |
| chef | *shefu* | シェフ |
| librarian | *toshogakari* | 図書係 |
| pilot | *pairotto* | パイロット |
| journalist | *kisha* | 記者 |
| comic book artist | *mangaka* | 漫画家 |
| graphic designer | *gurafikku dezainaa* | グラフィック　デザイナー |
| illustrator | *irasutoreetaa* | イラストレーター |
| waiter / waitress | *ueitaa / ueitoresu* | ウェイター／ウェイトレス |
| cleaner | *kurinaa / seisouin* | クリーナー　／清掃員 |

## *Listen to track 72*

## Places 場所  *basho*

| English | Romaji | Kana/Kanji |
|---|---|---|
| school | *gakkou* | 学校 |
| elementary school | *shougakkou* | 小学校 |
| junior high school | *chuugakkou* | 中学校 |
| high school | *koukou* | 高校 |
| university | *daigaku* | 大学 |
| classroom | *kyoushitsu / kurasuruumu* | 教室　/ クラスルーム |
| toilet | *toire* | トイレ |
| library | *toshokan* | 図書館 |
| hospital | *byouin* | 病院 |
| police station | *keisatsusho* | 警察署 |
| fire station | *shoubousho* | 消防署 |
| airport | *kuukou* | 空港 |
| my home | *uchi* | 家 |
| home / house | *ie* | 家 |
| cinema | *eigakan* | 映画館 |
| post office | *yuubinkyoku* | 郵便局 |

# Pronouns

While pronouns exist in Japanese, using the person's name to refer to them is more polite.

## *Listen to track 73*

| English | Romaji | Kanji/Kana |
|---|---|---|
| I / me | *watashi* | 私 |
| my | *watashi no* | 私の |
| you | *anata / kimi* | あなた / 君 |
| you (plural) | *anatatachi / kimitachi* | あなた達　/ 君たち |
| your | *anata no / kimi no* | あなた の　/ 君 の |
| they | *karera* | 彼ら |
| we / us | *watashitachi* | 私達 |
| our | *watashitachi no* | 私達 の |
| he / him | *kare* | 彼 |
| his | *kare no* | 彼の |

| she / her | *kanojo* | 彼女 |
| her (*possession*) | *kanojo no* | 彼女の |

## Honorifics

In Japanese there are honorifics used to show your relationship with the person you're talking to.

### *Listen to track 74*

-*san* is the most common honorific suffix.

-*chan* is used with girls or women that you are close friends with.

-*kun* is used to address boys or men that you are close friends with. Seniors in a company may use it to address their juniors.

-*sama* is used for people who hold an extremely high position such as God, king, queen, prince, and princess.

-*sensei* is used to address a teacher or doctor.

-*senpai* is used to address a senior at school or work.

## Kanji

### Writing basics

We looked at the kana and the stroke order in lesson 1 and a few kanji for numbers in lesson 2.

To make it easier to read, we have been including spaces between the kana.

However, when kanji is used there is no need for these spaces as it is easier to see where the words start and end.

### The basic rules for writing kanji

Start horizontal strokes first (from the left) then vertical strokes (from the top). Horizontal strokes are drawn left to right, and vertical strokes are drawn top to bottom. Diagonal strokes start at the top.

Note: There may be some exceptions to these rules.

Let's look at some basic verbs and their kanji.

## *Listen to track 75*

*kaku*

書く

write

| | | | | |
|---|---|---|---|---|
| | | | | |

*kiku*

聞く

listen / ask

| | | | | |
|---|---|---|---|---|
| | | | | |

*yomu*

読む

read

| | | | | |
|---|---|---|---|---|
| | | | | |

*hanasu*

話す

speak

| | | | | |
|---|---|---|---|---|
| | | | | |

*iu*

言う

say

|  |  |  |  |  |
|--|--|--|--|--|
|  |  |  |  |  |

*miru*

見る

see

|  |  |  |  |  |
|--|--|--|--|--|
|  |  |  |  |  |

*nomu*

飲む

drink

|  |  |  |  |  |
|--|--|--|--|--|
|  |  |  |  |  |

*taberu*

食べる

eat

|  |  |  |  |  |
|--|--|--|--|--|
|  |  |  |  |  |

*neru*

寝る

sleep

| | | | | |
|---|---|---|---|---|
| | | | | |

*go*

行く

go

| | | | | |
|---|---|---|---|---|
| | | | | |

*kuru*

来る

come

| | | | | |
|---|---|---|---|---|
| | | | | |

# Lesson activities

## Building sentences

### Exercise 1

Write these English phrases in romaji.

1. I am Takuya Yamada. _____
2. I am sixteen years old. _____
3. I am a university student. _____
4. I am Japanese. _____
5. My major is business. _____

### Exercise 2

Write these English phrases in romaji.

1. I have a pen. _____
2. Do you have a pencil? _____
3. I have a car. _____
4. Do you have a game console? _____
5. I don't have a laptop computer. _____

### Exercise 3

Write these English phrases in romaji.

1. I like cats. _____
2. I like dogs. _____
3. I don't like fish. _____
4. I don't like math. _____
5. Do you like English? _____

### Exercise 4

Write these English phrases in romaji

1. I am interested in science. _____
2. Are you interested in history? _____
3. I am not interested in politics. _____
4. Are you interested in politics? _____
5. I am interested in economics. _____

## Exercise 5

1. Do you like coffee? _____
2. Do you like sushi? _____
3. Do you like English? _____
4. Are you a student? _____
5. Are you Chinese? _____
6. Are you a nurse? _____
7. What's your favorite subject? _____
8. What is your major? _____
9. What is your job? _____
10. Where is the bank? _____
11. Where is the toilet? _____
12. Where is the post office? _____
13. When does the movie start? _____
14. When will you go to America? _____
15. When are you going to the office? _____
16. Why do you like English? _____
17. Who is that person? _____
18. Who is your teacher? _____

## Exercise 6

1. Introduce yourself. _____
2. Say what your nationality is. _____
3. Say that you are a university student. _____
4. Say that your major is Japanese. _____
5. Say you are a doctor. _____
6. Say that your father is a police officer. _____
7. Say that your mother is a lawyer. _____
8. Say that you like science. _____
9. Say that you don't like math. _____
10. Say that you are interested in the Korean language.

_____

## Exercise 7

Write these base verbs in kanji

1. *nomu*    _____
2. *taberu*  _____
3. *kaku*    _____
4. *yomu*    _____
5. *miru*    _____
6. *hanasu*  _____
7. *kiku*    _____
8. *neru*    _____
9. *kuru*    _____
10. *iku*    _____

## Answer key

### Exercise 1

Write these English phrases in romaji.

1. I am Takuya Yamada. <u>*Takuya Yamada desu.*</u>
2. I am sixteen years old. <u>*(watashi wa) juurokusai desu.*</u>
3. I am a university student. <u>*(watashi wa) daigakusei desu.*</u>
4. I am Japanese. <u>*(watashi wa) nihonjin desu.*</u>
5. My major is business. <u>*watashi no senkou wa bijinesu desu.*</u>

### Exercise 2

Write these English phrases in romaji.

1. I have a pen. <u>*(watashi wa )pen ga arimasu.*</u>
2. Do you have a pencil? <u>*enpitsu ga arimasu ka*</u>
3. I have a car. <u>*(watashi wa) kuruma ga arimasu.*</u>
4. Do you have a game console? <u>*geemuki ga arimasu ka.*</u>
5. I don't have a laptop computer. <u>*(watashi wa) nooto pasokon ga arimasen.*</u>

## Exercise 3

Write these English phrases in romaji.

1. I like cats. _neko ga suki desu._
2. I like dogs. _inu ga suki desu._
3. I don't like fish. _sakana ga suki dewa arimasen._
4. I don't like math. _sansuu ga suki dewa arimasen._
5. Do you like English? _eigo ga suki desu ka._

## Exercise 4

Write these English phrases in romaji.

1. I am interested in science. _kagaku ni kyoumi ga arimasu._
2. Are you interested in history? _rekishi ni kyoumi ga arimasu ka_
3. I am not interested in politics. _seiji ni kyoumi ga arimasen._
4. Are you interested in politics? _seiji ni kyoumi ga arimasu ka._
5. I am interested in economics. _seiji ni kyoumi ga arimasu._

## Exercise 5

Write these English phrases in romaji.

1. Do you like coffee? _koohii ga suki desu ka._
2. Do you like sushi? _sushi ga suki desu ka._
3. Do you like English? _eigo ga suki desu ka._
4. Are you a student? _gakusei desu ka._
5. Are you Chinese? _chuugokujin desu ka._
6. Are you a nurse? _kangoshi desu ka._
7. What's your favorite subject? _suki na kamoku wa nan desu ka._
8. What is your major? _senkou wa nan desu ka._
9. What is your job? _shigoto wa nan desu ka._
10. Where is the bank? _ginkou wa doko desu ka._
11. Where is the toilet? _toire wa doko desu ka._
12. Where is the post office? _yuubinkyoku wa doko desu ka._
13. When does the movie start? _eiga wa itsu hajimarimasu ka._
14. When will you go to America? _itsu amerika ni ikimasu ka._
15. When are you going to the office? _itsu kaisha ni ikimasu ka._
16. Why do you like English? _naze eigo ga suki desu ka._

17. Who is that person? *ano kata wa dare desu ka.*
18. Who is your teacher? *sensei wa dare desu ka.*

## Exercise 6

1. Introduce yourself. [name] + *desu.* (です)。
2. Say what your nationality is. country + *jin (人)*
3. Say that you are a university student. *watashi wa daigakusei desu.*
4. Say that your major is Japanese. *watashi no senkou wa nihongo desu.*
5. Say you are a doctor. *watashi wa isha desu.*
6. Say that your father is a police officer. *watashi no otousan wa keisatsukan desu.*
7. Say that your mother is a lawyer. *watashi no okaasan wa bengoshi desu.*
8. Say that you like science. *watashi wa kagaku ga suki desu.*
9. Say that you don't like math. *watashi wa sansuu ga suki ja arimasen. / watashi wa sansuu ga suki dewa arimasen.*
10. Say that you are interested in the Korean language. *watashi wa kankokugo ni kyoumi ga arimasu.*

## Exercise 7

Write these base verbs in kanji.

1. *nomu* 飲む
2. *taberu* 食べる
3. *kaku* 書く
4. *yomu* 読む
5. *miru* 見る
6. *hanasu* 話す
7. *iku* 聞く
8. *neru* 寝る
9. *kuru* 来る
10. *iku* 行く

## Listening script & answers

*Takuya: konnichiwa. amerikajin desu ka.*

たくや　こんにちは。アメリカ人　です　か。

Takuya: Hello. Are you American?

*Maria: iie, itariajin desu. gakusei desu ka.*

マリア: いいえ、イタリア人　です。学生ですか。

Maria: No, I am Italian. Are you a student?

*Takuya: hai, daigakusei desu.*

たくや: はい、大学生　です。

Takuya: Yes, I am a university student.

*Maria: sou desu ka. senkou wa nan desu ka.*

マリア: そう　です　か。せんこう　は　何　です　か。

Maria: I see. What is your major?

*Takuya: bijinesu desu.*

たくや: ビジネス　です。

Takuya: My major is business.

*Maria: sou desu ka. watashi no senkou wa nihongo desu. ryoushin no shigoto wa nan desu ka.*

マリア: そう　です　か。私　の　せんこう　は　日本語　です。りょうしん　の　しごと　は　何　です　か。

Maria: I see. What do your parents do?

*Takuya: otousan wa pairotto desu. okaasan wa isha desu.*

たくや: お父さん　は　パイロット　です。お母さん　は　医者　です。

Takuya: My father is a pilot. My mother is a doctor.

## Listen to the dialogue and answer the questions.

1. What nationality is Maria? <u>Italian</u>.
2. What is Maria's major? <u>Japanese</u>.
3. What is Takuya's major? <u>Business</u>.
4. What does Takuya's father do? <u>He's a pilot</u>.
5. What does Takuya's mother do? <u>She's a doctor.</u>

## Listen to the dialogue and answer the questions.

*Jyakku: Takuya-san wa nannin kazoku desu ka.*

ジャック: たくやさん　は　何人　かぞく　です　か。

*Jack: How many people are there in your family, Takuya?*

*Takuya: yonin kazoku desu. okaasan to otousan to otouto ga imasu.*

たきや: 四人　かぞく　です。お母さん　と　お父さん　と　弟　が　います。

*Takuya: There are four people in my family. I have a mother, father, and a little brother.*

*Jyakku: watashi wa otousan to otouto to oniisan ga imasu.*

ジャック: 私　は　お父さん　と　弟　と　お兄さん　が　います。

*Jack: I have a father, a little brother, and a big brother.*

*Takuya: Jyakku-san no otousan wa kuruma ga arimasu ka.*

たくや: ジャックさん　の　お父さん　は　くるま　が　あります　か。

*Takuya: Jack, does your father have a car?*

*Jyakku: iie, arimasen.*

ジャック: いいえ、ありません。

*Jack: No, he doesn't.*

1. How many people are in Takuya's family? <u>4 people</u>
2. Does Takuya have a little sister? <u>No</u>
3. How many people are in Jack's family? <u>4 people</u>
4. Does Jack have a little brother? <u>Yes</u>
5. Does Jack's father have a car? <u>No</u>

In this lesson, you will learn:

- How to say "this" and "that"
- Some common phrases
- The difference between *aru* and *iru*
- Particles *ne*, *yo*, *wa*, and *ga*
- How to ask for something
- Answering questions
- Asking "which...?"
- Hiragana – the *ka* row and *dakuten*
- Family members
- School objects

## Grammar

### *kore/sore/are & kono/sono/ano*

These words are used to express "this" and "that," depending on the position in the sentence and the location of the item in question.

### *Listen to track 76*

*kore / kono* - means "this" referring to an object near the speaker.

*kore* functions as a pronoun & *kono* functions as an adjective.

*sore / sono* - means "that" referring to an object near the listener.

*sore* functions as a pronoun & *sono* functions as an adjective.

*are / ano* - means "that" referring to an object that is near neither the speaker nor the listener.

*are* functions as a pronoun & *ano* functions as an adjective.

Compare the following sentences:

### Listen to track 77

kore wa watashi no pen desu.

これ は 私 の ぺん です。

This is my pen.

sore wa watashi no kaban desu.

それ は 私 の 鞄 です。

That is my bag.

are wa watashi no bento bako desu.

あれ は 私 の 弁当 箱 です。

That (over there) is my lunch box.

kono pen wa watashi no desu.

この ぺん は 私 の です。

This pen is mine.

sono kaban wa watashi no desu.

その 鞄 は 私 の です。

That bag is mine.

ano bento bako wa watashi no desu.

あの 弁当 箱 は 私 の です。

That lunch box (over there) is mine.

## Dialogue

### Listen to track 78

Takuya: katadzukemashoul

たくや: 片付けましょう

Takuya: Let's tidy up.

Riku: sou desu ne.

りく: そう です ね。

Riku: I agree.

Takuya: sono kutsu wa dare no desu ka.

たくや: その 靴 は 誰 の です か。

Takuya: Whose shoes are those?

Riku: Mitsuki-san no da to omoimasu.

りく: みつきさん の だ と 思います。

Riku: I think they are Mitsuki's.

Takuya: ano jaketto wa dare no desu ka.

たくや: あの ジャケット は 誰 の です か。

Takuya: Whose jacket is that?

Riku: Risa-san no da to omoimasu

りく: リサさん の だ と 思います。

Riku: I think it is Lisa's.

Takuya: kono paakaa wa dare no desu ka.

たくや: この パーカー は 誰 の です か。

Takuya: Whose hoodie is that?

Riku: Mitsuki-san no da to omoimasu.

りく: みつきさん の だ と 思います。

Riku: I think it's Mitsuki's.

## Grammar note:

*.....da to omoimasu* だ　と　思います　I think that....

*....*verb + *mashou* 〜ましょう　Let's.... (polite)

## Vocabulary:

*kutsu* 靴　shoes

*jaketto* ジャケット jacket

paakaa パーカー hoodie

## The particle *ne*　ね

*ne* is a particle that signals that you **agree** with the speaker or that you are **requesting confirmation or agreement**.

## Examples:

### *Listen to track 79*

*ashita, ame ga furimasu ne.*

明日、雨 が 降ります ね。

It's going to rain tomorrow, right?

*sou desu ne.*

そう　です　ね。

I agree with you.

*ikimashou ne.*

行きましょう　ね。

Let's go, shall we?

*ii desu ne.*

いい　です　ね。

Sounds good.

*kirei desu ne.*

綺麗　です　ね。

It's beautiful, isn't it?

## The Particle *wa*　は

In simple terms, **wa** is considered a **topic marker**.

When you use **wa**, both **you and the speaker are aware of the subject** being spoken about.

**Examples:**

**_Listen to track 80_**

_watashi no otouto wa yancha na ko desu._

私 の 弟 は やんちゃ な 子 です。

My little brother is a mischievous child.

_konshuu no shukudai wa muzukashii desu ne._

今週 の 宿題 は 難しい です ね。

This week's homework is difficult, isn't it?

_kurisumasu wa tanoshii desu._

クリスマス は 楽しい です。

Christmas is fun.

**Vocabulary:**

_otouto_ 弟　little brother

_yancha_ やんちゃ mischievous / naughty

_ko (domo)_ 子(ども) child

_konshuu_ 今週 this week

_shukudai_ 宿題 homework

_muzukashii_ 難しい difficult

_kurisumasu_ クリスマス Christmas

_tanoshii_ 楽しい fun

**Questions using _dochira_, _dore_ and _docchi_**

**_dore_** is a question word meaning "which" and is used when there are **three or more** objects to choose from.

**_docchi_** is a question word meaning "which" and is used when there are **two** objects to choose from.

**_dochira_** means the same as _docchi_ but is used in formal situations.

### *Listen to track 81*

## Examples:

*dore desu ka.*

どれ　です　か。

Which one is it?

*docchi ga hoshii? / docchi ga ii desu ka.*

どっち　が　欲しい。/ どっち　が　いい　です　か

Which one do you want?

*sansuu to kagaku to, dochira ga muzukashii desu ka.*

算数　と　科学　と、どちらが　難しい　です　か。

Which is more difficult, math or science?

## Vocabulary:

*hoshii* 欲しい　want

*ii* いい　good

*muzukashii* 難しい difficult

*kagaku* 科学　science

*sansuu* 算数 mathematics

# Speaking naturally

In Japanese it is common to remove the pronoun or subject from the sentence if it is obvious.

If anyone is unsure of what you are referring to, they are sure to ask for clarification by saying "Who is?" (*dare ga?*) or "What is?" (*nani ga?*).

## Example:

### *Listen to track 82*

*watashi no saifu wo nakushita > saifu wo nakushita*

私　の　財布　を　失くした　>財布　を　失くした

I lost my wallet > (I) lost (my) wallet.

## Vocabulary:

*nakusu* 失くす　to lose

*saifu* 財布 wallet

## Following the same pattern when answering

When answering a question formed with *ka*, simply remove the *ka* to make an affirmative answer or negate the verb to make a negative one. (We will look closer at negative conjugation in a later lesson.)

### *Listen to track 83*

*kodomo ga imasu ka.*

子供 が います か。

Do you have children?

*hai, kodomo ga imasu.*

はい、子供　が　います。

Yes, I have children.

*iie, kodomo ga imasen.*

いいえ、子供　が　いません。

No, I don't have children.

*Yamada-san desu ka.*

やまださん　です　か。

Are you Mr. Yamada?

*hai, Yamada desu.*

はい、やまだ　です。

Yes, I am Mr. Yamada.

*iie, Yamada-san ja arimasen.*

いいえ、やまださん　じゃ　ありません。

No, I am not Mr. Yamada.

*juurokusai desu ka.*

十六才　です　か。

Are you sixteen years old?

*hai, juurokusai desu.*

はい、十六才　です。

Yes, I am sixteen years old.

*iie, juurokusai ja arimasen.*

いいえ、十六才　じゃ　ありません。

No, I am not sixteen years old.

When answering a question formed with a *question word* and *ka,* replace the question word with a noun and remove *ka.*

### *Listen to track 84*

*nani wo motteimasu ka.*

何 を 持っています か。

What do you have?

*hon wo motteimasu.*

本 を 持っています。

I have a book.

*doko ni ikimasu ka.*

どこ に 行きます か。

Where are you going?

*toshokan ni ikimasu.*

図書館 に 行きます。

I'm going to the library.

*itsu ikimasu ka.*

いつ 行きます か。

When are you going?

*juuji ni ikimasu.*

十時 に 行きます。

I'm going at 10 o'clock.

*naze ikimasu ka.*

なぜ 行きます か。

Why are you going?

*eiga wo mi ni ikimasu.*

映画 を 見に行きます。

I am going to watch a movie.

*(kanojo wa) dare desu ka.*

「彼女 は」誰 です か。

Who is she?

*Maria-san desu.*

マリアさん です。

She's Maria.

## Useful phrases

### *Listen to track 85*

*chotto matte kudasai.*

ちょっと 待って ください

Please wait a moment.

*wakarimashita.*

分かりました

I understand.

*wakarimasen.*

分かりません

I don't understand. / I don't know.

*mou ichido itte kudasai.*

もう 一度 言って ください

Please say it one more time.

*yukkuri itte kudasai.*

ゆっくり 言って ください

Please speak slowly.

*shukudai wo dashite kudasai.*

宿題 を 出して ください。

Please hand in your homework.

*yamete kudasai.*

やめて　ください。

Please stop.

*machigatteimasu.*

間違っています。

It's not correct.

*eigo ga hanasemasu ka.*

英語　が　話せます　か。

Can you speak English?

*kono densha wa shibuya ni tomarimasu ka.*

この　電車　は　渋谷　に　止まります　か。

Does this train stop at Shibuya?

*shuuden wa nanji desu ka.*

終電　は　何時　です　か。

What time is the last train?

# Listening

Listen to the dialogue and answer the questions.

### *Listen to track 86*

1. What does Maria want to eat?        _____
2. What does Maria want to drink?      _____
3. Does Maria want dessert?            _____
4. How much did their purchase cost?   _____

# Vocabulary

### *Listen to track 87*

**Family 家族　*kazoku***

**Own family　自分　の　家族 *jibun no kazoku***

| English | Romaji | Kanji/Kana |
|---|---|---|
| mother | *okaasan / haha* (formal) | お母さん　/母 |
| mum | *mama* | ママ |
| father | *otousan / chichi* (formal) | お父さん　/父 |
| dad | *papa* | パパ |
| big brother | *oniisan / ani* (formal) | お兄さん　/兄 |
| little brother | *otouto* | 弟 |
| big sister | *oneesan / ane* (formal) | お姉さん　/姉 |
| little sister | *imouto* | 妹 |

| | | |
|---|---|---|
| siblings | *kyoudai* | 兄妹 |
| child | *uchi no ko* | うちの子 |
| daughter | *musume* | 娘 |
| son | *musuko* | 息子 |
| husband | *shujin / danna / otto* | 主人 ／旦那 ／夫 |
| wife | *kanai / tsuma / nyoubou* | 家内 ／妻 ／女房 |
| grandchild | *mago* | 孫 |
| grandmother | *obaasan / sobo* (formal) | おばあさん ／祖母 |
| grandfather | *ojiisan / sofu* (formal) | おじいさん ／祖父 |
| aunt | *obasan* | おばさん |
| uncle | *ojisan* | おじさん |
| cousin | *itoko* | いとこ |
| niece | *mei* | 姪 |
| nephew | *oi* | 甥 |

## Listen to track 88

# Someone else's family　他人のご家族 *tanin no go-kazoku*

| English | Romaji | Kanji/Kana |
|---|---|---|
| parents | *go-ryoushin* | ご両親 |
| mother | *okaasan* | お母さん |
| father | *otousan* | お父さん |
| siblings | *kyoudai* | 兄妹 |
| big brother | *oniisan* | お兄さん |
| little brother | *otoutosan* | 弟さん |
| big sister | *oneesan* | お姉さん |
| little sister | *imoutosan* | 妹さん |
| child | *o-kosan* | お子さん |
| son | *musukosan* | 息子さん |
| daughter | *musumesan* | 娘さん |
| husband | *go-shujin* | ご主人 |
| wife | *okusan* | 奥さん |
| grandmother | *obaasan* | おばあさん |
| grandfather | *ojiisan* | おじいさん |
| grandchild | *o-magosan* | お孫さん |
| aunt | *obasan* | おばさん |
| uncle | *ojisan* | おじさん |
| cousin | *itokosan* | いとこさん |

| niece | *meikkosan* | 姪っ子さん |
| nephew | *oikkosan* | 甥っ子さん |

## Listen to track 89

# School objects 学校の物　*gakkou no mono*

| English | Romaji | Kanji/Kana |
|---|---|---|
| table | *table* | テーブル |
| desk | *tsukue* | 机 |
| (ballpoint) pen | *(booru) pen* | 「ボール」ペン |
| pencil | *enpitsu* | 鉛筆 |
| eraser | *keshigomu* | 消しゴム |
| ruler | *jougi* | 定規 |
| pencil sharpener | *enpitsu kezuri* | 鉛筆削り |
| pencil case | *pen keesu / fudebako* | ペンケース / 筆箱 |
| paper | *kami* | 紙 |
| glue | *nori* | ノリ |
| scissors | *hasami* | ハサミ |
| highlighter | *keikou pen* | 蛍光ペン |
| notebook | *nooto* | ノート |
| textbook | *kyoukasho* | 教科書 |
| colored pencils | *iroenpitsu* | 色鉛筆 |
| backpack | *ryukku* | リュック |
| file | *fairu* | ファイル |
| marker | *maakaa* | マーカー |
| calculator | *dentaku* | 電卓 |

# Hiragana

## Exercise 1

Write these words as hiragana from the *k* row.

1. *kami* _____
2. *kaji* _____
3. *kiiro* _____
4. *kiku* _____
5. *kuro* _____

6. *kurai* _____
7. *keru* _____
8. *keshiki* _____
9. *kono* _____
10. *kore* _____

# Writing *ga* the correct way

## Exercise 2

All the characters have a specific stroke order. Take a closer look at **ga** and practice writing the listed words.

1. *gakkou* (school) _____
2. *gasshuku* (training camp) _____
3. *arigatou* (thanks) _____
4. *arigari* (crunchy) _____
5. *hiragana* _____
6. *kabushikigaisha* (corporation) _____
7. *higashi* (east) _____
8. *wagashi* (Japanese confectionery) _____
9. *gasshoudan* (choir group) _____
10. *gakkari* (disappointing) _____

## Dakuten

A **dakuten** looks like a quotation mark (") that changes the sound from voiceless to voiced.

## Examples:

### *Listen to track 90*

| | |
|---|---|
| *ka > ga* | *ta > da* |
| か ＞ が | た ＞ だ |
| *sa > za* | *ha > ba* |
| さ ＞ ざ | は ＞ ば |

## Practice

Try to say these words.

### *Listen to track 91*

*eiga* えいが

movie

*usagi* うさぎ

rabbit

*hagu* ハグ

hug

*hige* ひげ

mustache/beard

*eigo* えいご

English

*zasshi* ざっし

magazine

*kanji* かんじ

kanji

*shizuka* しずか

quiet

*zettai ni* ぜったいに

definitely

*zou* ゾウ

elephant

*dashi* だし

soup stock

*chidzhimu* ちぢむ

to shrink

*tsudzuku* つづく

to continue

*deru* でる

to come/go out

*doko* どこ

where

*baka* ばか

fool

*bikkuri* びっくり

surprise

*yobu* よぶ

to call

*yuube* ゆうべ

last night

*hobo* ほぼ

almost

# Lesson activities

## Sentence building

### Exercise 3

Write these sentences in romaji or kana/kanji. Use the vocabulary list to help you.

1. Coffee, please. _____
2. Green tea, please. _____
3. Pizza, please. _____
4. Which do you like, dogs or cats? _____
5. Which do you want, chocolate, vanilla, or strawberry? _____
6. Which is it? _____
7. You are a teacher, aren't you? _____
8. Let's go, shall we? _____
9. This is my pen. _____
10. That pen is mine. _____

## Answer key

## Hiragana

### Exercise 1

Write these words as hiragana from the *k* row.

1. *kami* かみ
2. *kaji* かじ
3. *kiiro* きいろ
4. *kiku* きく
5. *kuro* くろ
6. *kurai* くらい
7. *keru* ける
8. *keshiki* けしき
9. *kono* この
10. *kore* これ

### Exercise 2

1. *gakkou* (school) がっこう
2. *gasshuku* (training camp) がっしゅく
3. *arigatou* (thanks) ありがとう
4. *garigari* (crunchy) がりがり
5. *hiragana* ひらがな

6. *kabushikigaisha* (corporation) かぶしきがいしゃ

7. *higashi* (east) ひがし

8. *wagashi* (Japanese confectionery) わがし

9. *gasshoudan* (choir group) がっしょうだん

10. *gakkari* (disappointing) がっかり

## Exercise 3

Write these sentences in romaji or kana/kanji. Use the vocabulary list to help you.

1. Coffee, please.
   *koohi wo kudasai*
   コーヒー を ください

2. Green tea, please.
   *Ocha wo kudasai*
   おちゃ を ください

3. Pizza, please.
   *piza wo kudasai*
   ピザ を ください

4. Which do you like, dogs or cats?
   *inu to neko to, docchi ga suki desu ka.*
   いぬ と ネコ と、どっち が すき です か。

5. Which do you want, chocolate, vanilla, or strawberry?
   *chokoreeto to banira to ichigo , dore ga hoshii desu ka?*
   チョコレート と バニラ と いちご 、どれ が ほしい です か。

6. Which is it?
   *dore desu ka. / docchi desu ka.*
   どれ です か。/どっち です か。

7. You are a teacher, aren't you?
   *Sensei desu ne.*
   せんせい です ね。

8. Let's go, shall we?
   *ikimashou ne*
   いきましょう ね

9. This is my pen
   *kore wa watashi no pen desu.*
   これ は わたし の ぺん です。

10. That bag is mine.
    *sono kaban wa watashi no desu.*
    その かばん は わたし の です。

## Listening script & answers

*Takuya: Maria-san wa nani wo tabetai desu ka.*

たくや:マリアさん は 何 を 食べたい です か。

Takuya: What would you like to eat, Maria?

*Maria: chiizubaagaa wo tabetai desu.*

マリア: チーズバーガー を 食べたい です。

Maria: I would like to eat a cheeseburger.

*Takuya: nani wo nomitai desu ka.*

たくや: 何 を 飲みたい です か。

Takuya: What would you like to drink?

*Maria: koora wo nomitai desu.*

マリア: コーラ を 飲みたい です。

Maria: I would like to drink cola.

*Takuya: dezaato wo tabemasu ka.*

たくや: デザート を 食べます か。

Takuya: Are you going to eat dessert?

*Maria: iie, tabemasen.*

マリア: いいえ、食べません。

Maria: No, I won't.

*tenin: irrashaimase. gochuumon wo o-ukagai shimasu,*

店員: いらっしゃいませ。ご注文 を お伺い します。

Sales clerk: Welcome! I'll take your order.

*Takuya: eeto, chiizubaagaa futatsu to koora futatsu wo onegai shimasu.*

たくや: ええと、チーズバーガー　二つ　と　コーラ　二つ　を　お願い　します。

Takuya: Umm, two cheeseburgers and two colas, please.

*tenin: kashikomarimashita. happyakuen ni narimasu.*

店員: かしこまりました。800円　に　なります。

Sales clerk : Of course. That will be 800 yen.

## Listening

Listen to the dialogue and answer the questions.

1. What does Maria want to eat? <u>A cheeseburger</u>
2. What does Maria want to drink? <u>Cola</u>
3. Does Maria want dessert? <u>No</u>
4. How much did their purchase cost? <u>800 yen</u>

In this lesson, you will learn:

- How to say "who"
- How to make questions with question words
- How to turn statements into questions
- Talking about possession
- Hiragana - the "s" row
- Animal names

## Grammar

### The question word *dare* 誰

誰 *dare* is a question word meaning "who."

Let's look at some examples of how to build sentences using *dare*.

### Examples:

*Listen to track 92*

*ano kata wa dare desu ka.*

あの 方 は 誰 です か。

Who is that person?

*asoko no hito wa dare desu ka.*

あそこ の 人 は 誰 です か。

Who is that person over there?

*dare desu ka.*

誰 です か。

Who are you?

\* *kata* 方 is more polite than *hito* 人.

\* *ano* means *"that,"* referring to something or someone situated away from the speakers in the conversation and is followed by a noun.

\* *asoko* means "over there."

*dare* 誰 can be put with の to say "whose."

## Examples:

### *Listen to track 93*

*kore wa dare no wanpiisu desu ka.*

これ は 誰 の ワンピース です か。

Whose dress is this?

*korera wa dare no kutsu desu ka.*

これら は 誰 の 靴 です か。

Whose shoes are these?

*kono pen wa dare no desu ka.*

この ペン は 誰 の です か。

Whose pen is this?

*kono megane wa dare no desu ka.*

この メガネ は 誰 の です か。

Whose glasses are these?

## Assuming the topic based on context

The subject of the sentence can be removed if the subject is obvious.

## For example:

### *Listen to track 94*

東京 に 住んでいます

*Tokyo ni sundeimasu*

This literally means "living in Tokyo," but actually translates to "I live in Tokyo." In this case it is obvious that you are talking about yourself, so the pronoun *watashi* is omitted.

Take a look at this example dialogue.

## Vocabulary:

*okaasan* お母さん mother

*shokki* 食器　dishes

*kawakasanakya* 乾かさなきゃ (Base verb - *kawakasu* 乾かす to dry) have to dry (informal)

*totte* 取って (base verb *toru*　取る - to take) Please take. / Please get for me.

## Dialogue

### *Listen to track 95*

*okaasan: tsugi wa shokki wo kawakasanakya. Miyu-chan, are wo totte*

お母さん: 次　は　食器　を　乾かさなきゃ。みゆちゃん、あれ　を　取って。

Mother: Next, I have to dry the dishes. Miyu-chan, can you hand me that?

*Miyu: hai, mom.*

みゆ: はい、ママ。

Miyu: Yes, mom.

*are* あれ　means "that over there."

From the situation you can guess that Miyu-chan is being asked to get the towel to dry the dishes.

## Starting sentences with or without question words

### *Listen to track 96*

## "What" questions 何 (*nani*)

*nani wo shiteimasu ka*

何 を しています か。

What are you doing?

*shuumatsu ni nani wo shimasu ka.*

週末 に 何 を します か。

What are you going to do this weekend?

*suki na tabemono wa nan desu ka. / donna tabemono ga suki desu ka.*

好きな 食べ物 は 何 です か。/ どんな 食べ物 が 好き です か。

What food do you like?

*suki na nomimono wa nan desu ka. / donna nomimono ga suki desu ka.*

好きな 飲み物 は 何 です か。/ どんな 飲み物 が 好き です か。

What drink do you like?

*nani wo suru no ga suki desu ka.*

何 を する のが 好き です か。

What do you like to do?

## *Listen to track 97*

## "Where" questions どこ (*doko*)

*toire wa doko desu ka.*

トイレ は どこ です か

Where is the toilet?

*kyoushitsu wa doko desu ka.*

教室 は どこ です か。

Where is the classroom?

*toshokan wa doko desu ka.*

図書館 は どこ です か。

Where is the library?

*shokudou wa doko desu ka.*

食堂 は どこ です か。

Where is the cafeteria?

*resutoran wa doko desu ka.*

レストラン は どこ です か。

Where is the restaurant?

## Vocabulary:

toire トイレ　toilet

kyoushitsu 教室　classroom

toshokan 図書館　library

shokudou 食堂　cafeteria

resutoran レストラン restaurant

## Listen to track 98

## "When" questions いつ (*itsu*)

*itsu hajimarimasu ka.*

いつ　始まります　か。

When will it start?

*itsu owarimasu ka.*

いつ　終わります　か。

When will it end?

*itsu ikimasu ka.*

いつ　行きます　か。

When are you going?

*itsu shimasu ka.*

いつ　します　か。

When are you going to do it?

*itsu tsukimasu ka.*

いつ　着きます　か。

*When will you arrive?*

## Vocabulary:

*suru* する　*to do*

*hajimaru*　始まる *to start*

*owaru* 終わる　*to end*

*iku* 行く　*to go*

*tsuku* 着く　*to arrive*

## Listen to track 99

## "Why" questions なぜ　/ どうして / なんで ( *naze / doushite / nande* )

*naze shimashita ka.*

なぜ　しました　か。

Why did you do it?

*naze suki desu ka.*

なぜ　好き　です　か。

Why do you like it/them?

*naze ikimasu ka.*

なぜ　行きます　か。

Why are you going?

## Vocabulary:

*suki* 好き like

*iku* 行く　to go

## *Listen to track 100*

## "Who" questions 誰 (*dare*)

*dare desu ka*

誰　です　か。

Who are you?

*sensei wa dare desu ka.*

先生　は　誰　です　か。

Who is your teacher?

## *Listen to track 101*

## "How" questions どう ／どうやって （*dou / douyatte*）

*douyatte tsukaimasu ka*

どうやって　使います　か。

How do you use it?

*dou omoimasu ka.*

どう　思います　か。

What* do you think?

*douyatte ikimasu ka*

どうやって　行きます　か。

How do I get there?

*In this case the word "how" is used in Japanese, which often leads to Japanese speakers saying "How do you think?" in English.

## Exercise 1

Build these questions using the vocabulary list to help you.

*koko* ここ here

*imasu* います　to be (for people & living creatures)

*eigo* 英語 English

*eigakan* 映画館 cinema

*yuubinkyoku* 郵便局 post office

*toire* トイレ　toilet

*shimasu* します　to do (polite)

*shuumatsu* 週末 weekend

*sensei* 先生 teacher

*kanojo* 彼女　she/her

1. What are you doing on the weekend? _____
2. What is this? _____
3. What is that? _____
4. Where is the cinema? _____
5. Where is the toilet? _____
6. Where is the post office? _____
7. Who is she? _____
8. Who is your teacher? _____
9. Why do you like English? _____
10. Why are you here? _____

## "Are you" and "do you" questions

Putting *ka* at the end of a statement changes it into a question.

Compare the statements below.

### *Listen to track 102*

*kaishain desu.*

会社員　です。

I am an office worker.

*kaishain desu ka.*

会社員　です　か。

Are you an office worker?

*hatachi desu.*

二十歳　です。

I am 20 years old.

*hatachi desu ka.*

二十歳　です　か。

Are you 20 years old?

*okaasan wa isha desu.*

お母さん　は　医者　です。

My mother is a doctor.

*okaasan wa isha desu ka.*

お母さん　は　医者　です　か。

Is your mother a doctor?

*sakana ga suki desu.*

魚　が　好き　です。

I like fish.

*sakana ga suki desu ka.*

魚　が　好き　です　か。

Do you like fish?

*niku wo tabemasu.*

肉　を　食べます。

I eat meat.

*niku wo tabemasu ka.*

肉　を　食べます　か。

Do you eat meat?

## Listen to track 103

*Yamada desu.*

やまだ　です。

I am Mr.Yamada.

*Yamada-san desu ka.*

やまださん　です　か。

Are you Mr.Yamada?

*tenisu wo shimasu.*

テニス　を　します。

I play tennis.

*tenisu wo shimasu ka.*

テニス　を　します　か。

Do you play tennis?

*yakyuu wo suru no ga suki desu.*

野球　を　する　の　が　好き　です。

I like to play baseball.

*yakyuu wo suru no ga suki desu ka.*

野球　を　する　の　が　好き　です　か。

Do you like to play baseball?

*hon wo yomu no ga suki desu.*

本　を　読む　の　が　好き　です。

I like to read books.

*hon wo yomu no ga suki desu ka.*

本　を　読む　の　が　好き　です　か。

Do you like to read books?

*terebi wo miru no ga suki desu.*

テレビ　を　見る　の　が　好き　です。

I like to watch TV.

*terebi wo miru no ga suki desu ka.*

テレビ　を　見る　の　が　好き　です　か。

Do you like to watch TV?

## Vocabulary:

*terebi* テレビ　TV

*miru* 見る to watch

*hon* 本 book

*yomu* 読む to read

*yakyuu wo suru* 野球　を　する to play baseball

*tenisu wo suru* テニス　を　する to play tennis

## Exercise 2

Using the vocabulary list, build the sentences below.

*tenisu* テニス　tennis

*sakkaa* サッカー soccer

*yakyuu* 野球　baseball

*dansu wo suru (dansu wo shimasu)* ダンス　を　する (ダンス　を　します)　to dance

*geemu* ゲーム *game*

*hon wo yomu (hon wo yomimasu)* 本　を　読む (本　を　読みます) to read a book

*terebi wo miru (terebi wo mimasu)* テレビ　を　見る (テレビ　を　見ます) to watch TV

*juurokusai* 十六才 sixteen years old

*sakana* 魚　fish

*o-sake* お酒 alcohol

*taberu (tabemasu)* 食べる (食べます) to eat

*nomu (nomimasu)* 飲む (飲みます) to drink

*amerika* アメリカ America

*seito* 生徒 student

*kuruma* 車 car

*pen* ペン pen

1. Do you like tennis? _____
2. Do you like games? _____
3. Do you like soccer? _____
4. Do you like to dance? _____
5. Do you have a car? _____
6. Do you have a pen? _____
7. Do you eat fish? _____
8. Do you drink alcohol? _____
9. Are you 16 years old? _____
10. Are you a student? _____
11. Are you American? _____

12. Do you like to read books? _____

13. Do you like to watch TV? _____

## Possession

We have seen sentences in previous dialogues using the possessive "**no**" の。
This time, let's try to form some sentences.

## Making words possessive with the particle *no*

の is often translated as "of," but this can sound unnatural in English.
Take a look at the following examples.

## Examples:

### *Listen to track 104*

*watashi no namae*
私　の　名前
My name

*igirisu no koucha*
イギリス　の　紅茶
British tea

*nihon no touki*
日本　の　陶器
Japanese pottery

*nintendoo no Iwata-san*
ニンテンドー　の　岩田さん
Mr. Iwata of Nintendo

*amerika no furoridashuu*
アメリカ　の　フロリダ州
Florida in America

*toudai no seito*
東大　の　生徒
A student of Tokyo University

*koukou no sensei*
高校　の　先生
A high school teacher

*doitsu no isha*
ドイツ　の　医者
A doctor from Germany

## Exercise 3

Using the vocabulary list try to make the phrases using romaji.

**Vocabulary:**

*daigakusei* 大学生　university student

*shougakusei* 小学生　elementary school student

*chuugakusei* 中学生　junior high school student

*koukousei* 高校生 high school student

*amerika* アメリカ America

*oosutoraria* オーストラリア Australia

*furansu* フランス France

*supein* スペイン Spain

*itaria* イタリア　Italy

*igirisu* イギリス　U.K.

*isha* 医者 doctor

*bengoshi* 弁護士 lawyer

*sensei* 先生 teacher

*kome* 米 rice

*piza* ピザ pizza

*niku* 肉 meat

*sakana* 魚 fish

*ryouri* 料理　cuisine

1. French cuisine　_____
2. Italian pizza　_____
3. Japanese rice　_____
4. A teacher from Spain　_____
5. American meat　_____
6. An Australian junior high school teacher　_____
7. Japanese fish　_____
8. An American elementary school student　_____
9. A Japanese university student　_____
10. A British high school student　_____

## Showing possession of objects using no

**Pronoun + の + noun**

**_Listen to track 105_**

**Examples:**

_Maria no kuruma_

マリア　の　車

Maria's car

_yamada-san no nootopasokon_

やまださん　の　ノートパソコン

Yamada's laptop

_Takuya-san no enpitsu_

たくやさん　の　えんぴつ

Takuya's pencil

_Miyu-san no neko_

みゆさん　の　猫

Miyu's cat

_Mitsuki-san no shatsu_

みつきさん　の　シャツ

Mitsuki's shirt

_Riku-san no kaban_

りくさん　の　鞄

Riku's bag

_Hana-san no keitai (denwa)_

ハナさん　の　携帯 (電話)

Hannah's cell phone

## Exercise 4

Write these English phrases in romaji.

1. Takuya's dog _____
2. Jack's toothbrush _____
3. Mitsuki's bed _____
4. Maria's pajamas _____
5. Lisa's slippers _____
6. Hannah's teacher _____
7. Riku's school _____
8. Mr Sasaki's bag _____
9. Miss Nanase's laptop _____
10. Takuya's cell phone _____

# Hiragana

## The different versions of *sa* and *so*

When you see the hiragana character "**so**,", you may notice the shape is slightly different.

This "**so**" is written with one stroke and is commonly seen in print.

This "**so**" is written with two strokes and is commonly taught in the hiragana handwriting drills at school.

This "**sa**" is written with three strokes and is commonly taught in the hiragana handwriting drills at school.

This "**sa**" is written with two strokes and is commonly seen in print.

# Lesson activities

## Exercise 5

Write these words in hiragana.

1.  *sashimi*       _____
2.  *sakana*        _____
3.  *samishii*      _____
4.  *samui*         _____
5.  *sabaku*        _____

6.  *souji*         _____
7.  *soujiki*       _____
8.  *souryou*       _____
9.  *soumen*        _____
10. *sotsugyou*     _____

## Exercise 6

Write these phrases in English.

1.  *Takuya-san no neko*       _____
2.  *itaria no piza*          _____
3.  *nihon no kome*           _____
4.  *igirisu no koucha*       _____
5.  *sonii no Yoshida-san*    _____
6.  *watashi no pen*          _____
7.  *Takeshi-san no shatsu*   _____
8.  *amerika no isha*         _____
9.  *oosutoraria no niku*     _____
10. *furansu no ryouri*       _____

# Sentence building

## Exercise 7

Write these sentences and phrases in romaji.

1.  Do you have a pen?        _____
2.  Are you a teacher?        _____
3.  What do you like to do?   _____
4.  When is class?            _____
5.  Where is the classroom?   _____
6.  What do you think?        _____
7.  How do you use it?        _____
8.  Takeshi's hamster         _____
9.  A lawyer from Spain       _____

# Vocabulary

## *Listen to track 106*

## Animals 動物 *doubutsu*

| English | Romaji | Kana/Kanji |
|---|---|---|
| dog | *inu* | 犬 |
| cat | *neko* | 猫 |
| hamster | *hamusutaa* | ハムスター |
| bird | *tori* | 鳥 |
| goldfish | *kingyo* | 金魚 |
| guinea pig | *morumotto* | モルモット |
| rabbit | *usagi* | 兎 |
| mouse | *nezumi* | 鼠 |
| cow | *ushi* | 牛 |
| sheep | *hitsuji* | 羊 |
| pig | *buta* | 豚 |
| hen | *niwatori* | 鶏 |
| rooster | *ondori* | 雄鶏 |
| horse | *uma* | 馬 |
| snake | *hebi* | 蛇 |
| tiger | *tora* | 虎 |
| monkey | *saru* | 猿 |
| boar | *inoshishi* | 猪 |
| elephant | *zou* | 象 |
| lion | *raion* | ライオン |
| hippo | *kaba* | 河馬 |
| bat | *koumori* | コウモリ |

## Answer key

## Exercise 1

1. What are you doing on the weekend? *shuumatsu ni nani wo shimasu ka?*
2. What is this? *kore wa nan desu ka*
3. What is that? *are/sore wa nan desu ka.*
4. Where is the cinema? *eigakan wa doko desu ka.*
5. Where is the toilet? *toire wa doko desu ka.*

6. Where is the post office? *yuubinkyoku wa doko desu ka.*
7. Who is she? *kanojo wa dare desu ka. / ano kata wa dare desu ka.*
8. Who is your teacher? *sensei wa dare desu ka.*
9. Why do you like English? *naze eigo ga suki desu ka.*
10. Why are you here? *naze koko ni imasu ka.*

## Exercise 2

1. Do you like tennis? *tenisu ga suki desu ka.*
2. Do you like games? *geemu ga suki desu ka.*
3. Do you like soccer? *sakkaa ga suki desu ka.*
4. Do you like to dance? *dansu ga suki desu ka.*
5. Do you have a car? *kuruma ga arimasu ka.*
6. Do you have a pen? *pen ga arimasu ka.*
7. Do you eat fish? *sakana wo tabemasu ka.*
8. Do you drink alcohol? *o-sake wo nomimasu ka.*
9. Are you 16 years old? *juurokusai desu ka.*
10. Are you a student? *gakusei desu ka.*
11. Are you American? *amerikajin desu ka.*
12. Do you like to read books? *hon wo yomu no ga suki desu ka.*
13. Do you like to watch TV? *terebi wo miru no ga suki desu ka.*

## Exercise 3

1. French cuisine *furansu no ryouri / furansu ryouri*
2. Italian pizza *itaria no piza*
3. Japanese rice *nihon no kome*
4. A teacher from Spain *supein no sensei*
5. American meat *amerika no niku*
6. An Australian junior high school teacher *oosutoraria no chuugakkou no sensei*
7. Japanese fish *nihon no sakana*
8. An American elementary school student *amerika no shougakusei*
9. A Japanese university student *nihon no daigakusei*
10. A British high school student *igirisu no koukousei*

## Exercise 4

Write these English sentences in romaji.

1. Takuya's dog *Takuya-san no inu*
2. Jack's toothbrush *Jakku-san no haburashi*
3. Mitsuki's bed *Mitsuki-san no beddo*
4. Maria's pajamas *Maria-san no pajama*
5. Lisa's slippers *Risa-san no surippa*
6. Hannah's teacher *Hana-san no sensei*
7. Riku's school *Riku-san no gakkou*
8. Mr. Sasaki's bag *Sasaki-san no kaban*
9. Miss Nanase's laptop *Nanase-san no nooto pasokon*
10. Takuya's cell phone *Takuya-san no keitai (denwa)*

## Exercise 5

Write these words in hiragana.

1. sashimi さしみ
2. sakana さかな
3. samishii さみしい
4. samui さむい
5. sabaku さばく
6. souji そうじ
7. soujiki そうじき
8. souryou そうりょう
9. soumen そうめん
10. sotsugyou そつぎょう

## Exercise 6

Write these phrases in English.

1. *Takuya-san no neko* Takuya's cat
2. *itaria no piza* Italian pizza
3. *nihon no kome* Japanese rice
4. *igirisu no koucha* British tea
5. *sonii no Yoshida-san* Mr. Yoshida from Sony
6. *watashi no pen* My pen
7. *Takeshi-san no shatsu* Takashi's shirt
8. *amerika no isha* A doctor from America
9. *oosutoraria no niku* Australian meat
10. *furansu no ryouri* French cuisine

## Sentence building

### Exercise 7

Write these sentences and phrases in romaji.

1. Do you have a pen? _pen ga arimasu ka._
2. Are you a teacher? _sensei desu ka._
3. What do you like to do? _nani wo suru no ga suki desu ka._
4. When is class? _jugyou wa itsu desu ka._
5. Where is the classroom? _kyoushitsu wa doko desu ka._
6. What do you think? _dou omoimasu ka_
7. How do you use it? _douyatte tsukaimasu ka._
8. Takeshi's hamster _Takeshi-san no hamusutaa_
9. A lawyer from Spain _supein no bengoshi_

# Lesson 8: Colors and adjectives

In this lesson, you will learn:

- Colors
- The use of the particle "*to*"
- The use if the particle "*mo*"
- The use of the particle "*no*" to make adjectives
- More about the characters "*zu*" and "*ji*"

## Vocabulary

### Adjectives

*Listen to track 107*

| English | Romaji | Kanji |
|---------|--------|-------|
| good | *ii/yoi* | いい ／ 良い |
| new | *atarashii* | 新しい |
| old | *furui* | 古い |
| long | *nagai* | 長い |
| short | *mijikai* | 短い |
| round | *marui* | 丸い |
| square | *shikakui* | 四角い |
| big | *ookii* | 大きい |
| little | *chiisai* | 小さい |
| high | *takai* | 高い |
| low | *hikui* | 低い |
| early | *hayai* | 早い |
| late | *osoi* | 遅い |
| fast | *hayai* | 速い |
| slow | *osoi* | 遅い |

## *Listen to track 108*

## Colors 色　(*iro*)

| English | Romaji | Kanji |
|---------|--------|-------|
| red | *aka(i)* | 赤「い」 |
| orange | *orenji / daidaiiro* | オレンジ / 橙色 |
| yellow | *kiiro(i)* | 黄色「い」 |
| green | *midori* | 緑 |
| blue | *ao(i)* | 青「い」 |
| purple | *murasaki (iro)* | 紫 (色) |
| pink | *pink (iro) / momoiro* | ピンク　(色)　/ 桃色 |
| black | *kuro(i)* | 黒「い」 |
| white | *shiro(i)* | 白「い」 |
| brown | *chairo(i)* | 茶色「い」 |
| grey | *haiiro* | 灰色 |
| gold | *kiniro* | 金色 |
| silver | *giniro* | 銀色 |

**Note:**

When shopping you may notice that English names for colors are used and are written in katakana.

Black ブラック　*burakku*

White ホワイト *howaito*

Red レッド *reddo*

Blue ブルー *buruu*

Yellow イエロー *ieroo*

Green グリーン *guriin*

Brown ブラウン *buraun*

Grey グレー *guree*

Purple パープル *paapuru*

Gold ゴールド *goorudo*

Silver シルバー *shirubaa*

## Culture clip: Green is blue?

It is said that in the past, there was no word for "green" and green was considered a shade of "blue" 青　*ao*.

This is why you'll see some words using *ao* for objects that are obviously not blue, or green objects being referred to as *ao*. One of the most well-known being the *aoi shingou* 青い信号 blue traffic light.

Others include 青葉 (*aoba* blue leaves), 青芝 (*aoshiba* blue lawns) and 青りんご (*aoringo* blue apples).

# Grammar

## Talking about colors

Colors have a noun form and an adjective form.

The adjective forms are separated into "*i*" or "*no*" adjectives.

The primary colors - red, blue, yellow, black, white, and brown are "*i*" adjectives, the others are "*no*" adjectives.

**Examples:**

### Listen to track 109

*kuro* (noun form) black

*kuroi* (adj form) black

**"*i*" adj + noun**

*pinku* (noun form) pink

*pinku **no*** (adjective form) pink

### Listen to track 110

***kuroi neko*** 黒い　ネコ (black cat)

***akai tori*** 赤い　鳥 (red bird)

***aoi hana*** 青い　花 (blue flower)

*kore wa **shiroi hamusutaa** desu.*
これ　は　白い　ハムスター　です。
This is a **white hamster.**

*sore wa **kiiroi hana** desu.*
それ　は　黄色い　花　です。
That is a **yellow flower.**

**"*no*" adj + *no* + noun**

*are wa **chairoi uiggu** desu.*
あれ　は　茶色い　ウイッグ　です。
That is a **brown wig.**

### Listen to track 111

**orenji** no **hana** (orange flower)

オレンジ　の　花

**murasaki** no **wanpiisu** (purple dress)

紫　の　ワンピース

**pinku** no **kutsu** (pink shoes)

ピンク　の　靴

**noun + wa + adjective desu**

When we say "This [noun] is [color]," we use the form **noun + wa + adjective desu**. In this case the "i" and "no" should be dropped.

### Listen to track 112

kono **hana** wa **pinku** desu.

この　花　は　ピンク　です。

This **flower** is **pink.**

sono **megane** wa **ao** desu.

その　メガネ　は　青　です。

Those **glasses** are **blue**.

ano **kuruma** wa **aka** desu.

あの　車　は　赤　です。

That **car** is **red**.

## The particle *to*

The particle **to** is used for listing.

Look at the examples below.

### Listen to track 113

eigo **to** nihongo ga hanasemasu.

英語　と　日本語　が　話せます。

I can speak English **and** Japanese.

*hanasu* - speak *hanaseru* - can speak

*piano **to** baiorin ga hikemasu.*

ピアノ と バイオリン が 弾けます。

*I can play the piano **and** the violin.*

*\*hikeru - to be able to play a stringed instrument*

## The particle *mo*

The particle ***mo*** is used to say "**also.**"

### Listen to track 114

*watashi **mo** geemu ga suki desu.*

私 も ゲーム が 好き です。

I like video games **too**.

*\*suki* 好き like

*watashi **mo**.*

私 も

*Me **too***.

*kare **mo** kaze wo hiita.*

彼 も 風邪 を ひいた。

He **also** caught a cold.

*\*kaze* a cold

*\*kaze wo hiku* to catch a cold

# Hiragana

## Double consonants

Double consonants, known as *sokuon*, are represented by a small version of つ like this っ or in katakana like this ッ。

## Examples:

### Listen to track 115

*hotto suru* ほっとする

*hotto keeki* ホットケーキ

**Pronunciation tip: When you get to the double consonant you want to make a brief pause before saying the consonant.**

Practice saying these words:

### Listen to track 116

バット    *batto* baseball bat

雑誌 *zasshi* magazine

ゆっくり *yukkuri* slowly

行った *itta* went

サッカー *sakkaa* soccer

## ji or zhi じ・ ぢ / zu or dzu ず・ づ

In modern Japanese these characters are pronounced exactly the same:

### Listen to track 117

ず, づ can be pronounced [*dzu*] or [*zu*].

じ, ぢ can be pronounced [*dzi*] or [*ji*].

ぢ   and づ   were phased out of usage except for in certain conditions.

1. Repeated sound: 続く　つづく **tsudzuku** (continue), 縮む　ちぢむ **chidzimu** (shrink).
2. In words with *rendaku (an unvoiced syllable followed by a voiced syllable)*: 気づく　きづく **kidzuku** (to realize), 馬鹿力　ばかぢから **bakazikara** (enormous strength), お花茶屋駅　おはなぢゃや えき **ohanajaya eki** (Ohanajaya station).

These words can also be written with *ji* and *zu* in romaji:

*Nedzu* (ねづ) > *Nezu*

*\*Nezu* is a place name in Tokyo.

However, in order to make it easier to know which kana to write, this book romanizes the words with **dzi** and **dzu**.

# Lesson activities

## Exercise 1

Use the vocabulary to write the following phrases in romaji.

*ki* 木 tree        *seetaa* セーター sweater

*kiiro* 黄色 yellow        *shatsu* シャツ shirt

*ao* 青 blue        *murasaki* 紫 purple

*hana* 花 flower        *sukaato* スカート skirt

*pinku* ピンク pink        *basu* バス bus

*kuroi* 黒い black        *shiroi* 白い white

*chairoi* 茶色い brown        *kuruma* 車 car

*neko* 猫 cat        *enpitsu* 鉛筆 pencil

*midori* 緑 green        *akai* 赤い red

*inu* 犬 dog

1. Black cat   _____
2. Brown dog   _____
3. White shirt   _____
4. Red sweater   _____
5. Pink skirt   _____
6. This pencil is yellow _____
7. This car is blue   _____
8. This bus is green   _____
9. This flower is purple _____
10. This tree is brown   _____

## Building Sentences

## Exercise 2

Use the vocabulary to write these sentences in romaji.

*shiroi* 白い white        *nagai* 長い long

*ookii* 大きい big        *murasaki* 紫 purple

*chiisai* 小さい little        *takai* 高い expensive

*furui* 古い　old

*hako* 箱　box

*neko* 猫　cat

*kaban* 鞄　bag

*hana* 花　flower

*pen keesu* ペンケース　pencil case

*taoru* タオル　towel

*keitai* (*denwa*) 携帯　(電話) cell phone

*ie* 家　house

1. I have a white cat.　_____
2. I have a purple bag.　_____
3. I have a little flower.　_____
4. I have a long pencil case.　_____
5. I have a new box.　_____
6. I have an old towel.　_____
7. I have an expensive cell phone.　_____
8. I have a fast car.　_____
9. I have a big house.　_____

## Exercise 3

Write these words in *hiragana.*

1. *maji* (seriously?!)　_____
2. *chidzimu* (to shrink)　_____
3. *jikan* (time)　_____
4. *tsudzuku* (to continue)　_____
5. *jikoshoukai* (self introduction)　_____
6. *jidai* (era)　_____
7. *mikadzuki* (crescent moon)　_____
8. *kidzukai* (consideration for others)　_____
9. *kajiru* (to bite)　_____
10. *chuugokujin* (Chinese person)　_____

# Answer key

## Lesson activities

### Exercise 1

1. Black cat _kuroi neko_
2. Brown dog _chairoi inu_
3. White shirt _shiroi shatsu_
4. Red sweater _akai seetaa_
5. Pink skirt _pinku no sukaato_
6. This pencil is yellow. _kono enpitsu wa kiiro desu._
7. This car is blue. _kono kuruma wa ao desu._
8. This bus is green. _kono basu wa midori desu._
9. This flower is purple. _kono hana wa murasaki desu._
10. This tree is brown. _kono ki wa chairo desu._

## Building Sentences

### Exercise 2

1. I have a white cat. _shiroi neko ga imasu._
2. I have a purple bag. _murasaki no kaban ga arimasu._
3. I have a little flower. _chiisai hana ga arimasu._
4. I have a long pencil case. _nagai pen keesu ga arimasu,_
5. I have a new box. _atarashii hako ga arimasu._
6. I have an old towel _furui taoru ga arimasu._
7. I have an expensive cell phone. _takai keitai (denwa) ga arimasu._
8. I have a fast car. _hayai kuruma ga arimasu._
9. I have a big house. _ookii ie ga arimasu._

## Exercise 3

1. *maji* (seriously?!) <u>まじ</u>
2. *chidzimu* (to shrink) <u>ちぢむ</u>
3. *jikan* (time) <u>じかん</u>
4. *tsudzuku* (to continue) <u>つづく</u>
5. *jikoshoukai* (self introduction) <u>じこしょうかい</u>
6. *jidai* (era) <u>じだい</u>
7. *mikadzuki* (crescent moon) <u>みかづき</u>
8. *kidzukai* (consideration for others) <u>きづかい</u>
9. *kajiru* (to bite) <u>かじる</u>
10. *chuugokujin* (Chinese person) <u>ちゅうごくじん</u>

# Lesson 9: I like it!

In this lesson, you will learn:

- How to express likes and dislikes
- More adjectives
- How to express interest
- Hiragana practice - the *r* row

## Grammar

### Likes and dislikes

<u>**Listen to track 118**</u>

***X ga suki desu / X ga suki da***

***X ga suki dewa arimasen /X ga suki ja nai***

\*では   ***dewa*** can also be replaced by ***ja*** to make ***ja arimasen*** じゃ　ありません。

\*In informal speech the "***da***" is not really necessary and is dropped in natural speech.

**Examples:**

<u>**Listen to track 119**</u>

*geemu ga suki desu.*

ゲーム　が　好き　です。

I like games.

*murasaki ga suki.*

紫　が　好き。

I like purple.

*sakana ga suki dewa arimasen.*

魚　が　好き　では　ありません。

I don't like fish.

*kagaku ga suki.*

科学　が　好き。

I like science.

*sansuu ga suki ja nai.*

算数　が　好き　じゃ　ない。

I don't like math.

*inu to neko mo suki desu.*

犬　と　猫　も　好き　です。

I like dogs and cats.

126

*hebi ga suki ja arimasen.*

蛇 が 好き じゃ ありません。

I don't like snakes.

## Vocabulary:

*geemu* ゲーム game

*sakana* 魚 fish

*kagaku* 科学 science

*sansuu* 算数 math

*inu* 犬 dog

*neko* 猫 cat

*hebi* 蛇 snake

## Dialogue

### Listen to track 120

*Mitsuki: Takuya-san wa yakyuu ga jouzu desu ne. yakyuu ga suki desu ka.*

みつき: たくやさん は 野球 が 上手 です ね。野球 が 好き です か。

Mitsuki: Takuya, you're good at baseball, aren't you? Do you like baseball?

*Takuya: hontou wa, amari suki ja arimasen. sakkaa no hou ga suki desu.*

たくや: 本当 は、あまり 好き じゃ ありません。サッカー の 方 が 好き です。

Takuya: Actually, I don't like it very much. I prefer soccer.

*Mitsuki: watashi mo suki desu. kondo, issho ni sakkaa wo shimashou ne.*

みつき : 私 も 好き です。今度、一緒 に サッカー を しましょう ね。

Mitsuki: I also like it. Next time, let's play soccer together.

*Takuya: hai, zehi!*

たくや ; はい、是非

Takuya: Yes, I'd love to!

## Vocabulary:

*hontou wa* 本当 は actually

*amari* + ...nai/ ~masen あまり。。。ない/ません not very....

*no hou ga suki* の 方 が 好き　prefer

*issho ni* 一緒に　together

*zehi* 是非　certainly

## I like to…

### Listen to track 121

**X no ga suki desu / X no ga suki da.**

**X no ga suki de wa arimasen / X no ga suki ja nai**

## Examples:

### Listen to track 122

*yakyuu wo suru no ga suki desu.*

野球 を する の が 好き です。

I like playing baseball.

*hon wo yomu no ga suki desu.*

本 を 読む の が 好き です。

I like reading books.

*terebi wo miru no ga suki desu.*

テレビ を 見る の が 好き です。

I like watching TV.

*shousetsu wo kaku no ga suki desu.*

小説 を 書く の が 好き です。

I like writing novels.

*souji suru no ga suki dewa arimasen.*

掃除 する の が 好き では ありません。

I don't like cleaning.

*ryokou suru no ga suki dewa arimasen.*

旅行 する の が 好き では ありません。

I don't like traveling.

*benkyou suru no ga suki ja nai.*

勉強　する　の　が　好き　じゃ　ない

I don't like studying.

*kaimono suru no ga suki ja nai.*

買い物　する　の　が　好き　じゃ　ない

I don't like shopping.

## Vocabulary:

*yomu* 読む to read

*kiku* 聞く to listen/ask

*kaku* 書く to write

*miru* 見る to watch/look/see

*ryokou* 旅行 travel

*kaimono* 買い物 shopping

## I am interested in…

### *Listen to track 123*

**X ni kyoumi ga arimasu / X ni kyoumi ga arimasen**

**X ni kyoumi ga aru / X ni kyoumi ga nai (informal)**

## Examples:

### *Listen to track 124*

*rekishi ni kyoumi ga arimasu.*

歴史　に　興味　が　あります。

I am interested in history.

*densha ni kyoumi ga aru.*

電車　に　興味　が　ある。

I am interested in trains.

*kuruma ni kyoumi ga arimasen.*

車　に　興味　が　ありません。

I am not interested in cars.

*seiji ni kyoumi ga nai*

政治　に　興味　が　ない。

I am not interested in politics.

*ongaku ni kyoumi ga arimasu ka.*

音楽　に　興味　が　あります　か。

Are you interested in music?

## Vocabulary:

*rekishi* 歴史　history

*densha* 電車　train

*kuruma* 車　car

*seiji* 政治　politics

# Listening

Listen to the dialogue and answer the questions.

## *Listen to track 125*

1. Does Takuya like traveling?　_____
2. Does Lisa like traveling?　_____
3. Where has Takuya been?　_____
4. What does Lisa like to do on the plane?　_____
5. What does Takuya like to do on the plane? _____

## Vocabulary:

*omiyage* お土産　souvenir

*kau* 買う　to buy

*doitsu* ドイツ Germany

*igirisu* イギリス　U.K.

*hikouki* 飛行機　airplane

*eiga* 映画　movie

*miru* 見る　watch

*neru* 寝る　sleep

## Grammar note:

place + *itta koto arimasu ka* …. 行ったことありますか Have you been to…?

# Dialogue

## *Listen to track 126*

Hana: *Mitsuki-san wa ongaku ni kyoumi ga arimasu ka.*

ハナ: みつきさん　は　音楽　に　興味　が　あります　か。

Hannah: Mitsuki, are you interested in music?

Mitsuki: *hai, kyoumi ga arimasu. piano to baiorin ga hikemasu. Hana-san wa?*

みつき: はい、興味　が　あります。ピアノ　と　バイオリン　が　弾けます。
ハナさん　は？

Mitsuki: Yes, I am. I can play the piano and the violin. How about you?

*Hannah: piano to gitaa ga hikemasu.*

ハナ: ピアノ　と　ギター　が　弾けます。

Hannah: I can play the piano and the guitar.

*Mitsuki: kondo, issho ni konsaato wo mi ni ikimashou ne.*

みつき: 今度、一緒に コンサート を 見 に 行きましょう ね。

Mitsuki: Next time, let's go to a concert together.

*Hannah: ii desu ne.*

ハナ: いい　です　ね。

Hannah: Sounds good.

**Grammar note:**

*mi ni iku* 見　に　行く　*go to watch*

*hikeru* 弾ける　*can play (a stringed instrument)*

*konsaato* コンサート *concert*

# Speaking naturally

When pronouncing words like *kyoumi*, make sure to extend the "**ou**" sound to avoid being misunderstood. If you make the vowel sound too short, it will sound like a different word.

With sentences like ….***ga suki desu*** and ***…ga hoshii desu,*** the ***desu*** is omitted completely in informal language rather than being changed to its short form ***da***.

# Vocabulary

## New adjectives

### *Listen to track 127*

| English | Romaji | Kanji/Kana |
|---------|--------|------------|
| happy | *ureshii* | 嬉しい |
| sad | *kanashii* | 悲しい |
| pretty | *kirei (na)* | 綺麗　(な) |
| beautiful | *utsukushii* | 美しい |
| young | *wakai* | 若い |

| elderly | toshiyori / nenpai (no) | 年寄り （の）/ 年配 （の） |
| famous | yuumei (na) | 有名 （な） |
| important | taisetsu (na) | 大切 （な） |
| good at | jouzu (na) | 上手 （な） |
| bad at | heta (na) | 下手 （な） |
| interesting | omoshiroi | 面白い |
| fun | tanoshii | 楽しい |
| hate | kirai (na) | 嫌い |
| fortunate | saiwai | 幸い |

*some adjectives that end with the kana "*i*" are not conjugated like other "*i*" adjectives – **kirei**, **kirai**, and **saiwai** are those exceptions.

## <u>Listen to track 128</u>

# Sports and entertainment スポーツ と 娯楽 *supootsu to goraku*

| English | Romaji | Kana/Kanji |
|---|---|---|
| game | geemu | ゲーム |
| movie | eiga | 映画 |
| theater play | geki | 劇 |
| music | ongaku | 音楽 |
| radio | rajio | ラジオ |
| dance | dansu | ダンス |
| book | hon | 本 |
| karaoke | karaoke | カラオケ |
| singing | utau | 歌う |
| traveling | ryokou | 旅行 |
| festival | matsuri | 祭り |
| concert | konsaato | コンサート |
| comedy | o-warai | お笑い |
| soccer | sakkaa | サッカー |
| basketball | basukettobooru | バスケットボール |
| baseball | yakyuu | 野球 |
| tennis | tenisu | テニス |
| figure skating | figyua sukeeto | フィギュア　スケート |
| rugby | ragubii | ラグビー |
| volleyball | bareebooru | バレーボール |

| badminton | *badominton* | バドミントン |
| swimming | *suiei* | 水泳 |
| gymnastics | *taisou* | 体操 |
| cricket | *kuriketto* | クリケット |

**Listen to track 129**

## Fruit 果物 *kudamono*

| English | Romaji | Kana/Kanji |
|---|---|---|
| banana | *banana* | バナナ |
| orange | *orenji* | オレンジ |
| apple | *ringo* | りんご |
| grape | *budou* | ぶどう |
| strawberry | *ichigo* | 苺 |
| blueberry | *buruuberii* | ブルーベリー |
| raspberry | *razuberii* | ラズベリー |
| mango | *mangoo* | マンゴー |
| kiwi | *kiui* | キウイ |

# Hiragana

## Exercise 1

Write these words in hiragana.

1. *raishuu* (next week) _____
2. *rainen* (next year) _____
3. *rekishi* (history) _____
4. *retsu* (a row) _____
5. *rirekisho* (a resume) _____
6. *ryouri* (cuisine) _____
7. *roku* (six) _____
8. *rouka* (corridor) _____
9. *rusuban denwa* (answering machine) _____
10. *rui* (type) _____

# Lesson activities

## Sentence building

### Exercise 2

Write these words in English.

1. rekishi _____
2. densha _____
3. kuruma _____
4. seiji _____
5. omiyage _____

6. hikouki _____
7. neru _____
8. yomu _____
9. kau _____
10. kaku _____

### Exercise 3

Write these sentences in English.

1. karaoke ni kyoumi ga arimasu. _____
2. ongaku ni kyoumi ga arimasen. _____
3. rekishi ni kyoumi ga nai. _____
4. sakkaa ni kyoumi ga aru. _____
5. dansu wo suru no ga suki. _____
6. utau no ga suki ja nai. _____
7. hon wo yomu no ga suki desu. _____
8. chokoreeto ga suki desu. _____
9. banana ga suki dewa arimasen. _____
10. ichigo ga suki. _____

### Exercise 4

Write these sentences in romaji.

1. I like pizza. _____
2. I like basketball. _____
3. I don't like music. _____
4. I don't like mangoes. _____
5. I like to play soccer. _____
6. I don't like to play baseball. _____
7. I am interested in tennis. _____
8. I am not interested in politics. _____

## Answer key

## Listening script & answers

1.  Does Takuya like traveling? <u>Yes</u>
2.  Does Lisa like traveling? <u>Yes</u>
3.  Where has Takuya been? <u>Australia, Germany, and the U.K.</u>
4.  What does Lisa like to do on the plane? <u>She likes to watch movies.</u>
5.  What does Takuya like to do on the plane? <u>He likes to sleep.</u>

*Risa: Takuya-san wa ryokou suru no ga suki desu ka.*

リサ: たくや さん は 旅行 する の が 好き です か。

Lisa: Takuya, do you like traveling?

*Takuya: hai, suki desu. omiyage wo kau no ga suki desu.*

たくや: はい、好き です。お土産 を 買う の が 好き です。

Takuya: Yes, I do. I like to buy souvenirs.

*Risa: watashi mo suki desu. doko ni itta koto ga arimasu ka.*

リサ: 私 も 好き です。どこ に 行った こと が あります か。

Lisa: Me too. Where have you been?

*Takuya: oosutoraria to doitsu to igirisu ni itta koto ga arimasu.*

たくや: オーストラリア と ドイツ と イギリス に 行った こと が あります。

Takuya: I've been to Australia, Germany, and the U.K.

*Risa: ii desu ne. hikouki de eiga wo miru no ga suki desu. Takuya-san wa?*

リサ: いい です ね。飛行機 で 映画 を 見る の が 好き です。たくやさんは？

Lisa: That's nice. I like to watch movies on the plane. What about you?

*Takuya: neru no ga suki desu.*

たくや: 寝る の が 好き です。

Takuya: I like sleeping.

## Exercise 1

Write these words in hiragana.

1. *raishuu* <u>らいしゅう</u>
2. *rainen* <u>らいねん</u>
3. *rekishi* <u>れきし</u>
4. *retsu* <u>れつ</u>
5. *rirekisho* <u>りれきしょ</u>

6. *ryouri* <u>りょうり</u>
7. *roku* <u>ろく</u>
8. *rouka* <u>ろうか</u>
9. *rusuban denwa* <u>るすばん　でんわ</u>
10. *rui* <u>るい</u>

## Exercise 2

Write these words in English

1. *rekishi* <u>history</u>
2. *densha* <u>train</u>
3. *kuruma* <u>car</u>
4. *seiji* <u>politics</u>
5. *omiyage* <u>souvenir</u>

6. *hikouki* <u>plane</u>
7. *neru* <u>to sleep</u>
8. *yomu* <u>to read</u>
9. *kau* <u>to buy</u>
10. *kaku* <u>to write</u>

## Exercise 3

Write these sentences in English.

1. *karaoke ni kyoumi ga arimasu.* <u>I am interested in karaoke.</u>
2. *ongaku ni kyoumi ga arimasen.* <u>I am not interested in music.</u>
3. *rekishi ni kyoumi ga nai.* <u>I am not interested in history.</u>
4. *sakkaa ni kyoumi ga aru.* <u>I am interested in soccer.</u>
5. *dansu wo suru no ga suki.* <u>I like to dance.</u>
6. *utau no ga suki ja nai.* <u>I don't like to sing.</u>
7. *hon wo yomu no ga suki desu.* <u>I like to read books.</u>
8. *chokoreeto ga suki desu.* <u>I like chocolate.</u>
9. *banana ga suki dewa arimasen.* <u>I don't like bananas.</u>
10. *ichigo ga suki.* <u>I like strawberries.</u>

## Exercise 4

Write these sentences in romaji.

1. I like pizza. _piza ga suki desu._
2. I like basketball. _basukettobooru ga suki desu._
3. I don't like music. _ongaku ga suki dewa arimasen_
4. I don't like mangoes. _mangoo ga suki dewa arimasen_
5. I like to play soccer. _sakkaa wo suru no ga suki desu._
6. I don't like to play baseball. _yakyuu wo suru no ga suki dewa arimasen._
7. I am interested in tennis. _tenisu ni kyoumi ga arimasu._
8. I am not interested in politics. _seiji ni kyoumi ga arimasen._

# Lesson 10: How much is it?

In this lesson, you will learn:

- How to say "I want…" or "I don't want…"
- How to say something "is not ___" using adjectives
- Asking "How much?"
- Different ways of writing *fu*
- Transportation vocabulary

## Grammar

### Wanting and not wanting

**I want (something) / I don't want (something)**

*Listen to track 130*

*X ga hoshii desu / X ga hoshiku arimasen*

*X ga hoshii / X ga hoshikunai*

**Example:**

*Listen to track 131*

*geemuki ga hoshii.*

ゲーム機　が　欲しい。

I want a game console.

*pazuru ga hoshikunai.*

パズル　が　欲しくない

I don't want a puzzle.

*atarashii kaban ga hoshii desu.*

新しい　鞄　が　欲しい　です。

I want a new bag.

*yasai juusu ga hoshiku arimasen.*

野菜　ジュース　が　欲しく　ありません。

I don't want vegetable juice.

**I want to (do something) / I don't want to (do something)**

*X wo + verb + tai desu / X wo + verb + taku arimasen*

*X wo + verb + tai / X wo + verb + takunai*

Note: in the case of "become," "come," "meet," and "go" the particle *ni* is used.

## Examples:

### *Listen to track 132*

*geemu wo shitai.*

ゲーム を したい。

I want to play games.

*gakkou ni ikitakunai.*

学校 に 行きたくない。

I don't want to go to school.

*okanemochi ni naritai.*

お金持ち に なりたい。

I want to be rich.

*hourensou wo tabetaku arimasen.*

ほうれん草 を 食べたく ありません。

I don't want to eat spinach.

# Culture clip

## Invitations

Although in English we use "Do you want to…" or "Would you like to..." to invite people, Japanese questions with " verb + *tai*" should not be used for invitations.

In these cases, we should use the negative form of the verb.

### *Listen to track 133*

*issho ni eigakan ni ikimasen ka*

一緒 に 映画館 に 行きません か。

Would you like to go to the cinema with me?

# New adjectives

### *Listen to tracks 134 and 135*

| English | Romaji | Kanji/Kana |
|---|---|---|
| good | *yoi / ii* | 良い/いい |
| pretty | *kirei* | きれい |
| delicious | *oishii* | 美味しい |
| awful | *mazui* | 不味い |
| scary | *kowai* | 怖い |
| cute | *kawaii* | 可愛い |
| dangerous | *abunai* | 危ない |
| busy | *isogashii* | 忙しい |
| amazing | *sugoi* | 凄い |

| cool | kakkoii | かっこいい |
|---|---|---|
| kind | yasashii | 優しい |
| fun | tanoshii | 楽しい |
| wonderful | subarashii | 素晴らしい |
| horrible | hidoi | ひどい |
| lame | dasai | ダサい |
| bad | warui | 悪い |
| boring | tsumaranai | つまらない |
| awful | iya | 嫌 |
| wrong | machigatta | 間違った |
| tall (person's height) | se ga takai | 背　が　高い |
| short (person's height) | se ga hikui | 背　が　低い |
| wide | hiroi | 広い |
| narrow | semai | 狭い |
| fat | futotteiru | 太っている |
| thin | hosoi | 細い |
| heavy | omoi | 重い |
| light | karui | 軽い |
| shallow | asai | 浅い |
| deep | fukai | 深い |
| far | tooi | 遠い |
| near | chikai | 近い |
| quiet | shizuka | 静か |
| safe | anzen | 安全 |
| free | hima | 暇 |

# Grammar

## Making adjectives negative

*i adj + ku arimasen / i adj + kunai (informal)*

### Listen to track 136

*sono doubutsu wa kawaikunai.*

その　動物　は　可愛くない。

That animal is not cute.

*ano hana wa utsukushikunai.*

あの　花　は　美しくない。

That flower is not pretty.

*kono puuru wa fukaku arimasen.*

この　プール　は　深く　ありません。

*This pool is not deep.*

*o-bake wa kowakunai.*

お化け　は　怖くない。

Ghosts are not scary.

*watashi no inu wa abunaku arimasen.*

私　の　犬　は　危なく　ありません。

My dog is not dangerous.

**na adj + dewa (ja) arimasen / na adj + ja nai (informal)**

**_Listen to track 137_**

*kono wanpiisu wa kirei ja nai.*

この　ワンピース　は　綺麗　じゃ　ない。

This dress is not pretty.

*watashi wa hima ja nai.*

私　は　暇　じゃ　ない。

I am not free.

*ano basho wa shizuka dewa arimasen.*

あの　場所　は　静か　では　ありません。

That place is not quiet.

*watashi ga umareta machi wa anzen ja arimasen.*

私　が　生まれた　町　は　安全　じゃ　ありません。

The town where I was born is not safe.

## The colors as negative adjectives

The colors follow the same rules as regular *i* and *na* adjectives above.

**Examples:**

*i* **adjectives**

### Listen to track 138

*kuroku arimasen.*

黒く　ありません。

It's not black.

*shiroku arimasen.*

白く　ありません。

It's not white.

*akakunai.*

赤くない。

It's not red.

*no* **adjective**

### Listen to track 139

*pinku ja nai.*

ピンク　じゃ　ない。

It's not pink

*orenji dewa arimasen.*

オレンジ　では　ありません。

It's not orange

*midori ja arimasen.*

緑　じゃ　ありません。

It's not green.

## Tricky uses of the particle *no*

### noun + *no*

By putting a noun or an adjectival noun with *no*, it can be used to describe an object or person.

### Listen to track 140

*mahou no kagi.*

魔法　の　鍵。

A magic key

*midori no kurumaisu.*

緑　の　車椅子。

A green wheelchair

*honto no shiawase.*

本当　の　幸せ。

true happiness

*byouki no hito.*

病気　の　人。

a sick person

## adj + *no*

*no* can also be used to mean "one" where the subject is obvious.

### Listen to track 141

*akai no ga hoshii.*

赤い　の　が　欲しい。

I want the red one.

*murasaki no ga suki.*

紫　の　が　好き。

I like the purple one.

*tairyou no toiretto peepaa.*

大量 の トイレット ペーパー。

a lot of toilet paper

*ookii no ga hoshii.*

大きい　の　が　欲しい。

I want the big one.

*chiisai no ga suki.*

小さい　の　が　好き。

I like the small one.

## Vocabulary:

*ookii* 大きい　big

*chiisai* 小さい small

## *no* for positions

### Listen to track 142

*no* can also be used with prepositions when telling location.

*on 上　*ue* / in 中　*naka* / under 下 *shita* / by そば　*soba*

*beddo no shita.*

ベッド　の　下

under the bed.

*tsukue no ue.*

机　の　上

on the desk.

143

isu no soba.

椅子　の　そば

by the chair.

hako no naka.

箱　の　中

in the box.

## Numbers and money

### How much…?

You can see in the dialogue below that *o-ikura desu ka* is used to ask "How much?"

The "o" in *o-ikura* is optional, but sounds more polite.

### Dialogue:

### *Listen to track 143*

*Maria: ano pinku no sukaato wa o-ikura desu ka.*

マリア: あの　ピンク　の　スカート　は　おいくら　です　か。

Maria: How much is the pink skirt?

*tenin: nisen en desu.*

店員: 二千 円　です。

Sales clerk: It's 2,000 yen.

*Maria: ano akai boushi wa o-ikura desu ka.*

マリア: あの　赤い　帽子　は　おいくら　です　か。

Maria: How much is the red hat?

*tenin: dochira no akai boushi ga yoroshii deshou ka.*

店員: どちら　の　赤い　帽子　が　宜しい　でしょう　か。

Sales clerk: Which red hat would you like?

*Maria: ookii no wo kudasai.*

マリア: 大きい の　を　ください

Maria: The big one please.

*tenin: happyaku en desu.*

店員: 八百円　です。

Sales clerk: It's 800 yen.

*Maria: kono sukaato to boushi wo onegai shimasu.*

マリア: この　スカート　と　帽子　を　お願いします。

Maria: This skirt and this hat please.

*tenin: nisenhappyaku en ni narimasu.*

店員: 二千八百 円 に なります。

Sales clerk: That will be 2,800 yen.

*Maria: hai.*

マリア: はい。

Maria: Here you are.

*tenin: gosen en wo azukari shimasu. nisennihyaku en okaeshi desu. doumo arigatou gozaimashita*

店員: 五千 円 を 預かり します。二千二百円 お返し です。どうも　ありがとうご ざいました。

Sales clerk: I have received 5,000 yen. That's 2,200 yen change. Thank you very much.

## Listening

Listen to the dialogue and answer the questions.

### *Listen to track 144*

**Vocabulary:**

*chekku* チェック checkered

*mizutama* 水玉　polkadot

1. How much is the skirt? _____
2. How much is the sweater? _____
3. How much was the total cost? _____
4. How much change did she get? _____

# Hiragana

## What is that circle?

The small circle that you see above some letters is called a *handakuten*.

It changes the pronunciation of the **h** row of the kana chart to a **p** sound.

## Practice

Say these words with the *handakuten*.

### Listen to track 145

*piza* ピザ

*painappuru* パイナップル

*pinku* ピンク

## Exercise 1

Write these words with handakuten.

1. *sanpo (a walk)* _____
2. *pittari (exact)* _____
3. *tenpo (store branch)* _____

## Why isn't *fu* written as *hu*?

The pronunciation of ふ falls between an f and h sound, with the teeth behind the bottom lip while voicing *hu*.

## Practice

Say these words with **fu**.

### Listen to track 146

*fumu* ふむ (to stand on)

*fumin* ふみん (insomnia)

*futatsu* ふたつ (two)

*haafu* ハーフ (half)

*furansu* フランス (France)

*furadansu* フラダンス (Hula dance)

## The easy way to write *fu*

This is the stroke order for ふ in hiragana:

However, the first and second strokes and even the third and fourth strokes can be joined together in one stroke to make writing it faster.

## Exercise 2

Write these words in hiragana from the "h" row.

1. *hana* (nose / flower) _____
2. *haru* (spring) _____
3. *hima* (not busy) _____
4. *hisashiburi* (long time no see) _____
5. *hebi* (snake) _____
6. *heiki* (fine) _____
7. *houhou* (method) _____
8. *homeru* (to praise) _____
9. *fuyu* (winter) _____
10. *furu* (to shake) _____

# Lesson activities

## Sentence building

### Exercise 3

Write these phrases in English.

1. *geemuki ga hoshii.* _____
2. *pazuru ga hoshikunai.* _____
3. *atarashii kaban ga hoshii desu.* _____
4. *sono doubutsu wa kawaikunai.* _____
5. *ano hana wa utsukushikunai.* _____
6. *kono wanpiisu wa kirei ja nai.* _____
7. *watashi wa hima ja nai.* _____
8. *sofa no shita.* _____
9. *tansu no naka. tansu** 箪笥   *chest of drawers _____
10. *pasokon no ue.* _____
11. *beddo no soba.* _____
12. *murasaki no ga hoshii.* _____
13. *ookii no ga watashi no. ookii** 大きい   *big _____
14. *mahou no tobira. tobira** 扉   *door _____
15. *pinku no heddohon.** ヘッドホン *headphones. _____

### Exercise 4

Write these phrases in romaji.

**vocabulary:**

*toshokan* library

*toranpetto* trumpet

*utau* sing (**verb stem**: *utai*)

1. I don't want vegetable juice. _____
2. I don't want a trumpet. _____
3. I want pizza. _____
4. I want to go to the library. _____
5. I want to sing. _____
6. This pool is not deep. _____

7. Ghosts are not scary. _____

8. My dog is not dangerous. _____

9. That place is not quiet. _____

10. I am not busy. _____

11. I want the blue one. _____

12. Under the bed. _____

13. On the desk. _____

14. By the chair. _____

15. In the box. _____

## Exercise 5

Write these prices in kanji.

1. 800 yen _____    6. 50 yen _____

2. 100 yen _____    7. 5000 yen _____

3. 500 yen _____    8. 1 yen _____

4. 1000 yen _____   9. 10,000 yen _____

5. 10 yen _____    10. 2,500 yen _____

# Vocabulary

## Listen to track 147

## Transportation 交通 *koutsuu*

| English | Romaji | Kanji/Kana |
|---|---|---|
| car | *kuruma* | 車 |
| bicycle | *jitensha* | 自転車 |
| motorbike | *baiku* | バイク |
| bus | *basu* | バス |
| train | *densha* | 電車 |
| plane | *hikouki* | 飛行機 |
| boat | *fune* | 船 |
| taxi | *takushii* | タクシー |
| helicopter | *heri* | ヘリ |
| truck | *torakku* | トラック |

## Answer key

## Listening

Listen to the dialogue and answer the questions.

## Listening script:

*Maria: ano akai chekku no sukaato wa o-ikura desu ka.*

マリア: あの　赤い　チェック　の　スカート　は　おいくら　です　か。

Maria: How much is the red checkered skirt?

*tenin: gosen en desu.*

店員: 五千 円　です。

Sales clerk: It's 5,000 yen.

*Maria: ano murasaki no mizutama no seetaa wa o-ikura desu ka.*

マリア: あの　紫　の　水玉　の　セーター　は　おいくら　です　か。

Maria: How much is the purple polkadot sweater?

*tenin: sanzen en desu.*

店員: 三千 円　です。

Sales clerk: It's 3,000 yen.

*Maria: kono sukaato to seetaa wo onegai shimasu.*

マリア: この　スカート　と　セーター　を　お願いします。

Maria: This skirt and this hat please.

*tenin: hassen en ni narimasu.*

店員: 八千円 に　なります。

Sales clerk: That will be 8,000 yen.

*Maria: hai.*

マリア: はい。

Maria: Here you are.

*tenin: ichiman en wo azukari shimasu. nisen en okaeshi desu. doumo arigatou gozaimashita*

店員: 一万　円 を 預かり します。二千 円 お返し です。どうも　ありがとう ございました。

Sales clerk: I have received 10,000 yen. That's 2,000 yen change. Thank you very much.

1. How much is the skirt? <u>5,000 yen.</u>
2. Which sweater does she want? <u>The purple polkadot sweater.</u>
3. How much is the sweater? <u>3,000 yen.</u>
4. How much was the total cost? <u>8,000 yen.</u>
5. How much change did she get? <u>2,000 yen.</u>

## Exercise 1

Write these words with handakuten.

1. *sanpo* <u>さんぽ</u>
2. *pittari* <u>ぴったり</u>
3. *tenpo* <u>テンポ</u>

## Exercise 2

Write these words in hiragana.

1. *hana* <u>はな</u>
2. *haru* <u>はる</u>
3. *hima* <u>ひま</u>
4. *hisashiburi* <u>ひさしぶり</u>
5. *hebi* <u>へび</u>
6. *heiki* <u>へいき</u>
7. *houhou* <u>ほうほう</u>
8. *homeru* <u>ほめる</u>
9. *fuyu* <u>ふゆ</u>
10. 10. *furu* <u>ふる</u>

## Exercise 3

Write these phrases in English.

1. *geemuki ga hoshii.* <u>I want a game console.</u>
2. *pazuru ga hoshikunai.* <u>I don't want a puzzle.</u>
3. *atarashii kaban ga hoshii desu.* <u>I want a new bag.</u>
4. *sono doubutsu wa kawaikunai.* <u>That animal is not cute.</u>
5. *ano hana wa utsukushikunai.* <u>That flower is not beautiful.</u>
6. *kono wanpiisu wa kirei ja nai.* <u>That dress is not pretty.</u>

7. *watashi wa hima ja nai.* <u>I am not free.</u>
8. *sofa no shita* <u>Under the sofa</u>
9. *tansu no naka* <u>In the chest of drawers</u>
10. *pasokon no ue* <u>On the PC</u>
11. *eddo no soba* <u>By the bed</u>
12. *murasaki no ga hoshii* <u>I want the purple one.</u>
13. *ookii no ga watashi no.* <u>The big one is mine.</u>
14. *mahou no tobira* <u>A magic door</u>
15. *pinku no heddohon* <u>Pink headphones</u>

## Exercise 4

Write these phrases in romaji.

1. I don't want vegetable juice. *yasai juusu wa hoshikunai /hoshiku arimasen.*
2. I don't want a trumpet. *toranpetto wa hoshikunai /hoshiku arimasen.*
3. I want pizza. *piza ga hoshii (desu).*
4. I want to go to the library. *toshokan ni ikitai (desu).*
5. I want to sing. *utaitai (desu).*
6. This pool is not deep. *kono puuru wa fukaku nai / arimasen.*
7. Ghosts are not scary. *obake wa kowaku nai / arimasen.*
8. My dog is not dangerous. *watashi no inu wa abunaku nai / arimasen.*
9. That place is not quiet. *ano basho wa shizuka janai / dewa arimasen.*
10. I am not busy. *(watashi wa) isogashi kunai / ku arimasen.*
11. I want the blue one. *aoi no ga hoshii (desu).*
12. Under the bed *beddo no shita*
13. On the desk *tsukue no ue*
14. By the chair *isu no soba*
15. In the box *hako no naka*

## Exercise 5

Write these prices in kanji.

1. 800 yen <u>八百円</u>
2. 100 yen <u>百円</u>
3. 500 yen <u>五百円</u>
4. 1,000 yen <u>千円</u>
5. 10 yen <u>十円</u>

6. 50 yen <u>五十円</u>
7. 5,000 yen <u>五千円</u>
8. 1 yen <u>一円</u>
9. 10,000 yen <u>一万円</u>
10. 2,500 yen <u>二千五百円</u>

# Lesson 11: Where is it?

In this lesson, you will learn:

- Places vocabulary
- How to say where something is
- Adjectives
- Use of the particle *yo*
- *wa* vs. *ga*
- The particle *mo*

## Grammar

**Where is….?**

***Listen to track 148***

⌒ *doko desu ka* どこ です か。

*~wa doko ni arimasu ka / wa doko ni imasu ka* ～は どこ に あります か /～はどこ に います か。

**It is….**

⌒ *ni imasu/* ⌒ *ni arimasu* どこ に あります ／どこ に います

The verb ***iru*** and ***aru*** (to be) can be used to say where someone or something is.

**Examples:**

***Listen to track 149***

*Maria-san wa doko desu ka.*

マリアさん は どこ です か。

Where is Maria.

*(Maria-san wa) kyoushitsu ni imasu.*

「マリアさん は」 教室 に います。

(Maria is) in the classroom.

*Takuya-san wa doko ni imasu ka.*

たくやさん は どこ に います か。

Where is Takuya?

*(Takuya-san wa) shokudou ni imasu.*

「たくやさん」は 食堂 に います。

(Takuya is) in the cafeteria.

*kuukou wa doko desu ka.*

空港 は どこ です か。

Where is the airport?

*(kuukou wa) shoppingu mooru no tonari\* ni arimasu.*

(空港 は) ショッピングモール の 隣 に あります。

(The airport) is next to the shopping center.

*tonari* 隣  next to

*watashi no pasupooto wa doko desu ka.*

私 の パスポート は どこ です か。

Where is my passport?

*(anata no pasupooto wa) tsukue no hikidashi\* no naka\* ni arimasu.*

(あなた の パスポート は) 机 の 引き出し の 中 に あります。

(Your passport is) in the desk drawer.

*hikidashi* 引き出し  drawer

*naka* 中 inside

*suupaa wa doko ni arimasu ka.*

スーパー は どこ に あります か。

Where is the supermarket?

*(suupaa wa) yuubinnkyoku no mukaigawa\* ni arimasu.*

(スーパー　は) 郵便局　の　向かい側　に　あります。

(The supermarket is) across from the post office.

*\*mukaigawa* 向かい側　across from

## Prepositions

As seen in lesson 10, the particle *no* should come between the object and the preposition.

### *Listen to track 150*

*ue* 上 on/above

*naka* 中 in

*shita* 下 under

*soba* そば by

*tonari* 隣　next to

*mae* 前　in front of

*ushiro* 後ろ behind

## Examples:

### *Listen to track 151*

*neko wa sofa no **ue** ni imasu.*

猫　は　ソファ　の　上　に　います。

The cat is on the sofa.

*hon wa hako no **naka** ni arimasu.*

本　は　箱　の　中　に　あります。

The book is in the box.

*inu wa teeburu no **shita** ni imasu.*

犬　は　テーブル　の　下　に　います。

The dog is under the table.

*kaban wa isu no **soba** ni arimasu.*

鞄　は　椅子　の　そば　に　あります。

The bag is by the chair.

*Maria-san wa Takuya-san no **tonari** ni imasu.*

マリアさん は たくやさん の 隣 に います。

Maria is next to Takuya.

*sofa no **mae** ni teeburu ga arimasu.*

ソファ の 前 に テーブル が あります。

There is a table in front of the sofa.

*beddo no **ushiro** ni ranpu ga arimasu.*

ベッド の 後ろ に ランプ が あります。

There is a lamp behind the bed.

### Listen to track 152

**dokoka どこか　somewhere**

*dokoka ni arimasu.*

どこか に あります。

It's somewhere.

*dokoka ni ikimashou.*

どこか に 行きましょう。

Let's go somewhere.

### Listen to track 153

**dokonimo どこにも + negative verb　nowhere/anywhere**

*watashi no saifu wa doko ni mo nai.*

私 の 財布 は どこ に も ない

My wallet isn't anywhere.

*otouto wa doko ni mo inai*

弟 は どこ に も いない。

My brother isn't anywhere.

### Listen to track 154

**dokodemo どこでも wherever**

*makku wa dokodemo aru.*

マック は どこでも ある。

McDonald's is everywhere.

*dokodemo ii*

どこでも いい

Wherever is fine.

*doko ni ikou ka.*

どこ に 行こう か

Where should we go?

## Particle yo よ

**yo** is a particle used to strengthen your words and assure the listener that what you say is true.

**Examples:**

### *Listen to track 155*

*kono shukudai wa muzukashii desu yo.*

この　宿題　は　難しい　です　よ。

This homework is difficult.

*watashi wa amerikajin dewa arimasen yo.*

私　は　アメリカ人　では　ありません　よ。

I am not American.

*abunai* yo.

危ない　よ。

Watch out!

*ki wo tsukete yo.*

気　を　つけて　よ。

Please be careful.

*tasukete yo!*

助けて　よ！

Help me!

### *wa* vs. *ga*

In simple terms, **wa** is considered a **topic marker** and **ga** is considered a **subject marker.**

When you use **ga**, you are **introducing a subject** into the conversation that wasn't being spoken about at that time. It can also be used to **emphasize** or to **request information.**

When you use **wa**, both **you and the speaker are aware of the subject** being spoken about.

The example sentence below is commonly used to help make the usage clearer.

### Listen to track 156

*mukashimukashi, ojiisan to obaasan **ga** sundeimashita.*

*ojiisan to obaasan **wa** totemo shinsetsu deshita.*

昔々、おじいさん と おばあさん が 住んでいました。

おじいさん とおばあさん は とても 親切で した。

Once upon a time, there was **an** old man and an old woman.

**The** old man and the old woman were very kind.

**More examples:**

### Listen to track 157

*piza ga tabetai desu.*

ピザ　が　食べたい　です。

I want to eat pizza (very much).

*onigiri wa suki desu ka.*

おにぎり　は　すき　です　か。

Do you like rice balls?

*hai, onigiri ga daisuki desu.*

はい、おにぎり　が　大好き　です。

Yes, I love rice balls.

*dare ga watashi no keeki wo tabemashita ka.*

誰　が　私　の　ケーキ　を　食べました　か。

Who ate my cake?

**Vocabulary:**

*mukashi mukashi* 昔々 Long ago / Once upon a time

*ojiisan* おじいさん old man / grandfather

*obaasan* おばあさん old woman / grandmother

*to* と　and

*totemo* とても very

*shinsetsu* 親切 kind

*deshita* でした　was/were

## The particle "mo" も　- also /too

### Listen to track 158

*mo* follows the subject to mean "**too.**"

Compare the following sentences:

*kore wa watashi no pen desu.*

これ　は　私　の　ペン　です。

This is my pen.

*sore wa watashi no kaban desu.*

それ　は　私　の　鞄　です。

That is my bag.

*kore **mo** watashi no pen desu.*

これ　も　私　の　ぺん　です。

This is my pen too.

*sore **mo** watashi no kaban desu.*

それ　も　私　の　鞄　です。

That is my bag too.

# Vocabulary

### Listen to track 159

## Locations 場所　basho

| English | Romaji | Kana/Kanji |
|---|---|---|
| train station | *eki* | 駅 |
| bus stop | *basu tei* | バス 停 |
| airport | *kuukou* | 空港 |
| hotel | *hoteru* | ホテル |
| clinic | *kurinikku* | クリニック |
| hospital | *byouin* | 病院 |
| pharmacy | *yakkyoku* | 薬局 |
| drug store | *doraggu sutoa* | ドラッグ ストア |
| factory | *koujou* | 工場 |
| park | *kouen* | 公園 |

| bakery | *panya* | パン屋 |
| book store | *honya* | 本屋 |
| post office | *yuubinkyoku* | 郵便局 |
| Japanese inn | *ryokan* | 旅館 |
| room | *heya* | 部屋 |
| office | *jimusho* | 事務所 |
| company | *kaisha* | 会社員 |
| workplace | *shokuba* | 職場 |
| hot spring | *onsen* | 温泉 |
| city hall | *shiyakusho* | 市役所 |

## New adjectives

### Listen to track 160

| English | Romaji | Kanji/Kana |
|---|---|---|
| hot | *atsui* | 熱い |
| hot (weather) | *atsui* | 暑い |
| cold | *tsumetai* | 冷たい |
| cold (weather) | *samui* | 寒い |
| soft | *yawarakai* | 柔らかい |
| hard | *katai* | 硬い |
| spicy | *karai* | 辛い |
| salty | *shoppai* | しょっぱい |
| sweet | *amai* | 甘い |
| funny | *omoshiroi* | 面白い |
| shy | *uchiki* | 内気 |
| intelligent | *atama ga ii* | 頭 が いい |
| energetic | *genki* | 元気 |
| brave | *yuuki ga aru* | 勇気 が ある |
| friendly | *shinsetsu* | 親切 |
| curious | *koukishin ga aru* | 好奇心 が ある |
| polite | *teinei* | 丁寧 |
| honest | *shoujiki* | 正直 |

## *Listen to track 161*

## More animals　もっと　動物　*motto doubutsu*

| English | Romaji | Kana/Kanji |
|---|---|---|
| goat | *yagi* | ヤギ |
| bear | *kuma* | 熊 |
| gorilla | *gorira* | ゴリラ |
| raccoon | *araiguma* | アライグマ |
| polar bear | *shirokuma* | 白熊 |
| dolphin | *iruka* | イルカ |
| squid | *ika* | イカ |
| whale | *kujira* | 鯨 |
| octopus | *tako* | タコ |
| ant | *ari* | アリ |
| bee | *hachi* | 蜂 |
| spider | *kumo* | クモ |
| alligator | *wani* | ワニ |
| camel | *rakuda* | ラクダ |
| frog | *kaeru* | カエル |
| crab | *kani* | カニ |
| kangaroo | *kangaruu* | カンガルー |
| koala | *koara* | コアラ |
| snake | *hebi* | 蛇 |

# Mini conversation

## Vocabulary:

*massugu itte* 真っ直ぐ 行って go straight

*migi ni magatte* 右 に 曲がって turn right

*hidari ni magatte* 左 に 曲がって turn left

*mukaigawa* 向かい側 across from

*tonari* 隣　next to

*shiyakusho* 市役所 city hall

*byouin* 病院 hospital

*basutei* バス停 bus stop

*suupaa* スーパー supermarket

*eki* 駅 station

### Listen to track 162

*Risa: sumimasen. basu tei wa doko desu ka.*

リサ：すみません。バス停はどこですか。

Lisa: Excuse me. Where is the bus stop?

*Lady: massugu itte, migi ni magatte, suupaa no mukaigawa ni arimasu.*

女の人：真っ直ぐ行って、右に曲がって、スーパーの向かい側にあります。

Lady: Go straight, turn right, and it's opposite the supermarket.

*Risa: arigatou gozaimasu.*

リサ: ありがとうございます。

Lisa: Thank you.

# Listening

## Listening 1

### Listen to track 163

Listen to the dialogue and answer the questions.

1. Where does Lisa want to go?
2. Which way does she have to turn?
3. What building is next to her destination?

## Listening 2

### Listen to track 164

Listen to the dialogue and answer the questions.

1. Where does Lisa want to go?
2. Which way does she have to turn?
3. What building is opposite her destination?

# Hiragana

| n | w– | r– | y– | m– | h– | n– | t– | s– | k– | |
|---|---|---|---|---|---|---|---|---|---|---|
| ん N | わ WA | ら RA | や YA | ま MA | は HA | な NA | た TA | さ SA | か KA | あ A | –a |
| | ゐ WI | り RI | | み MI | ひ HI | に NI | ち CHI | し SHI | き KI | い I | –i |
| | | る RU | ゆ YU | む MU | ふ FU | ぬ NU | つ TSU | す SU | く KU | う U | –u |
| | ゑ WE | れ RE | | め ME | へ HE | ね NE | て TE | せ SE | け KE | え E | –e |
| | を WO | ろ RO | よ YO | も MO | ほ HO | の NO | と TO | そ SO | こ KO | お O | –o |

# Lesson activities

## Exercise 1

Write these words from the m-row.

1. *maru* (circle) _____
2. *majime* (diligent) _____
3. *mimi* (ears) _____
4. *miru* (to see) _____
5. *murasaki* (purple) _____
6. *mune* (chest) _____
7. *megane* (glasses) _____
8. *unten menkyo* (driver's license) _____

## Exercise 2

Write these sentences in romaji.

1. I like sushi too. _____
2. Be careful. _____
3. Where is Takuya? _____
4. Takuya is at the supermarket. _____
5. Where is the toilet? _____
6. It's across from the classroom. _____
7. Where is the train station? _____
8. It's next to the post office. _____
9. Turn right. _____
10. Go straight. _____

## Exercise 3

Write these sentences in English.

1. *watashi mo neko ga suki desu.* _____
2. *watashi mo anime ga suki desu.* _____
3. *kuukou wa doko desu ka.* _____
4. *byouin wa doko desu ka.* _____
5. *hoteru wa doko desu ka.* _____
6. *yuubinkyoku no tonari ni arimasu.* _____

7. *yakkyoku no mukaigawa ni arimasu.* _____
8. *panya no migigawa ni arimasu.* _____
9. *honya no hidarigawa ni arimasu.* _____
10. *hidari ni magatte.* _____

## Exercise 4

Write these phrases in English.

1. *hamusutaa wa teeburu no **ue** ni imasu.* _____
2. *sakkaa booru wa kaban no **naka** ni arimasu.* _____
3. *kaban wa teeburu no **shita** ni arimasu.* _____
4. *neko wa isu no **soba** ni imasu.* _____
5. *Mitsuki wa Risa no **tonari** ni imasu.* _____
6. *beddo no **mae** ni hako ga arimasu.* _____
7. *sofa no **ushiro** ni neko ga imasu.* _____
8. *teeburu no **ue** ni banana ga arimasu.* _____
9. *isu no **ue** ni taoru ga arimasu.* _____
10. *beddo no **tonari** ni teeburu ga arimasu.* _____

## Exercise 5

Write these phrases in romaji.

1. The book is on the table. _____
2. The cell phone is in the bag. _____
3. The dog is under the table. _____
4. The bag is by the chair. _____
5. Lisa is next to Hanako. _____

## Answer key

## Listening script and answers

## Listening 1

*Risa: sumimasen. eki wa doko desu ka.*

リサ：すみません。駅　は どこ です か。

Lisa: Excuse me. Where is the station?

*Lady: massugu itte, hidari ni magatte, shiyakusho no tonari ni arimasu.*

女の人: 真っ直ぐ 行って、左 に 曲がって、市役所 の 隣 に あります。

Lady: Go straight, turn right, and it's next to the city hall.

*Risa: arigatou gozaimasu.*

リサ: ありがとう ございます。

Lisa: Thank you.

1. Where does Lisa want to go? <u>The station</u>.
2. Which way does she have to turn? <u>Left</u>.
3. What building is next to her destination? <u>The city hall.</u>

## Listening 2

*Risa: sumimasen. byouin wa doko desu ka.*

リサ：すみません。病院　は どこ です か。

Lisa: Excuse me. Where is the hospital?

*Lady: massugu itte, hidari ni magatte, gakkou no mukaigawa ni arimasu.*

女の人: 真っ直ぐ 行って、左 に 曲がって、学校 の 向かい側 に あります。

Lady: Go straight, turn left, and it's opposite the school.

*Risa: arigatou gozaimasu.*

リサ: ありがとう ございます。

Lisa: Thank you.

1. Where does Lisa want to go? <u>The hospital.</u>
2. Which way does she have to turn? <u>Left.</u>
3. What building is opposite her destination? <u>The school.</u>

## Exercise 1

Write these words from the m-row.

1. *maru* <u>まる</u>
2. *majime* <u>まじめ</u>
3. *mimi* <u>みみ</u>
4. *miru* <u>みる</u>
5. *murasaki* <u>むらさき</u>
6. *mune* <u>むね</u>
7. *megane* <u>めがね</u>
8. *unten   menkyo* <u>うんてん　めんきょ</u>

## Exercise 2

Write these sentences in romaji.

1. I like sushi too. _watashi mo sushi ga suki desu._
2. Be careful. _ki wo tsukete yo_
3. Where is Takuya? _Takuya-san wa doko desu ka._
4. Takuya is at the supermarket. _Takuya-san wa suupaa ni imasu._
5. Where is the toilet? _toire wa doko desu ka._
6. It's across from the classroom. _kyoshitsu no mukaigawa ni arimasu._
7. Where is the train station? _eki wa doko desu ka._
8. It's next to the post office. _yuubinkyoku no tonari ni arimasu._
9. Turn right. _migi ni magatte_
10. Go straight. _massugu itte_

## Exercise 3

Write these sentences in English.

1. _watashi mo neko ga suki desu._ I like cats too
2. _watashi mo anime ga suki desu._ I like anime too.
3. _kuukou wa doko desu ka._ Where is the airport.
4. _byouin wa doko desu ka._ Where is the hospital?
5. _hoteru wa doko desu ka._ Where is the hotel?
6. _yuubinkyoku no tonari ni arimasu._ It's next to the post office.
7. _yakkyoku no mukaigawa ni arimasu._ It's opposite the pharmacy.
8. _panya no migigawa ni arimasu._ It's to the right of the bakery.
9. _honya no hidarigawa ni arimasu._ It's to the left of the book store.
10. _hidari ni magatte._ Turn left.

## Exercise 4

Write these phrases in English.

1. _hamusutaa wa teeburu no ue ni imasu._ The hamster is on the table.
2. _sakkaa booru wa kaban no naka ni arimasu._ The soccer ball is in the bag.
3. _kaban wa teeburu no shita ni arimasu._ The bag is under the table.
4. _neko wa isu no soba ni imasu._ The cat is by the chair.
5. _Mitsuki wa Risa no tonari ni imasu._ Mitsuki is next to Lisa.
6. _beddo no mae ni hako ga arimasu._ There is a box in front of the bed.

7. *sofa no ushiro ni neko ga imasu.* <u>There is a cat behind the sofa.</u>
8. *teeburu no ue ni banana ga arimasu.* <u>There is a banana on the table.</u>
9. *isu no ue ni taoru ga arimasu.* <u>There is a towel on the chair.</u>
10. *beddo no tonari ni teeburu ga arimasu.* <u>There is a table next to the bed.</u>

## Exercise 5

Write these phrases in romaji.

1. The book is on the table *hon wa teeburu no ue ni arimasu.*
2. The cell phone is in the bag. *keitai denwa wa kaban no naka ni arimasu.*
3. The dog is under the table. *inu wa teeburu no shita ni imasu.*
4. The bag is by the chair. *kaban wa isu no soba ni arimasu.*
5. Lisa is next to Hanako. *Risa-san wa Hanako-san no tonari ni imasu.*

# Lesson 12: It's sunny today

In this lesson, you will learn:

- Holidays in Japan
- The weather
- Food and drink
- Adjectives
- Dates
- Time expressions
- Verbs
- Expressing the past
- The usage if the particle *wo*

## Culture clip: Christmas and other holidays in Japan

### Christmas & New Year

### *Listen to track 165*

Christmas is celebrated a little differently than in other countries. Having a Christmas tree is becoming increasingly common. However, many Japanese people eat KFC, pizza, and sponge cake on the night of Christmas Eve.

On Boxing Day, all Christmas decorations are taken down in order to put up the New Year decorations.

New Year decorations often include the zodiac animal of the upcoming year and many are made of rope, bamboo, and pine. It is considered bad luck to put up decorations last minute on the 31st and also on the 29th since the pronunciation of 9 (*ku*) sounds like 苦 (*ku*) meaning "suffering."

On New Year's Eve, eating **o-sechi** & **toshikoshi soba** is common. On New Year's Day, a soup called o-zoni which has mochi in it is commonly eaten.

People travel to the shrines to pray for good fortune for the New Year in what is known as **hatsumode**.

## Hina Matsuri

*Hina Matsuri,* also known as "Girls' Day," is held on March 3rd and is a holiday that commemorates the happiness, prosperity, and growth of girls.

On this day, families with girls display special Hina dolls on steps. These dolls are extremely expensive, so they are usually passed down through generations.

Colorful food such as **chirashizushi**, **hina-arare,** and Hina doll cakes are eaten.

## Children's Day

Children's Day, also known as Boys' Day, is celebrated on May 5th to celebrate boys and recognize fathers.

Koi carp streamers and *Kabuto* are the traditional decorations of this occasion. The Koi streamers represent prayers for the healthy growth of boys, and the Kabuto symbolizes strength and vitality.

Commonly eaten food includes *Kashiwa Mochi* and *Chimaki.*

## Tanabata

*Tanabata,* also known as the Star Festival, originates from a Chinese story where the two stars Altair and Vega separated by the Milky Way are able to meet once again.

It's tradition to write a wish on a long piece of paper and tie it to a bamboo tree.

## Obon

*Obon* is celebrated in mid-August from the 13th to the 16th to commemorate one's ancestors.

*Obon* dance festivals are held, and many people return to the site of their ancestors' graves.

# Vocabulary

## Talking about the weather

Use the phrase *o-tenki wa dou desu ka* to ask "How's the weather?"

Tenki 天気 means weather. The "o" is optional, but sounds more polite.

### Listen to track 166

***hare*** *desu.*

晴れ　です。

It's **sunny**.

***kumori*** *desu.*

曇り　です。

It's **cloudy**.

*kyou no tenki wa* ***ame*** *desu.*

今日　の　天気　は　雨　です。

Today's weather is **rainy**.

*ashita\* no tenki wa* ***yuki*** *desu.*

明日　の　天気　は　雪　です。

Tomorrow's weather will be **snowy**.

*\*ashita* 明日　tomorrow

*kinou\* no tenki wa* ***arashi*** *deshita.*

きのう　の　天気　は　嵐　でした。

There was a **storm** yesterday.

*\*kinou* 昨日 yesterday

*kinou,* ***kaze*** *wa tsuyokatta desu.*

きのう、風　は　強かった　です。

The **wind** was strong yesterday.

### Listen to track 167

**More weather words** もっと　天気　の　単語　*motto tenki no tango*

| English | Romaji | Kana/Kanji |
|---|---|---|
| typhoon | *taifuu* | 台風 |
| low air pressure | *teikiatsu* | 低気圧 |
| degrees (Celsius)* | *do* | 度 |
| hail (big) | *hyou* | 雹 |
| hail (small) | *arare* | 霰 |

*Temperature in Japan is measured in Celcius not Fahrenheit. 20度　*niijuudo* 20 degrees C

171

## *Listen to track 168*

# Food and drink 食べ物　と　飲み物 *tabemono to nominomo*

| English | Romaji | Kana/Kanji |
|---|---|---|
| water | *mizu* | 水 |
| black tea | *koucha* | 紅茶 |
| green tea | *ocha* | お茶 |
| barley tea | *mugicha* | 麦茶 |
| oolong tea | *uurongucha* | 烏龍茶 |
| coffee | *koohii* | コーヒー |
| cocoa | *kokoa* | ココア |
| milk | *gyuunyuu* | 牛乳 |
| rice | *gohan / kome* | ご飯　/ 米 |
| hamburger | *hanbaagaa* | ハンバーガー |
| chicken | *toriniku / chikin* | 鶏肉　/ チキン |
| beef | *gyuuniku / biifu* | 牛肉　/ ビーフ |
| pork | *butaniku / pooku* | 豚肉　/ ポーク |
| vegetables | *yasai* | 野菜 |
| salad | *sarada* | サラダ |
| tomato | *tomato* | トマト |
| cucumber | *kyuuri* | キュウリ |
| lettuce | *retasu* | レタス |
| carrot | *ninjin* | ニンジン |
| cabbage | *kyabetsu* | キャベツ |
| spinach | *hourensou* | ほうれん草 |
| green beans | *ingen* | インゲン |
| mushrooms | *kinoko* | キノコ |

## *Listen to track 169*

# Months 月 *tsuki*

| English | Romaji | Kana/Kanji |
|---|---|---|
| January | *ichigatsu* | 一月 |
| February | *nigatsu* | 二月 |
| March | *sangatsu* | 三月 |
| April | *shigatsu* | 四月 |
| May | *gogatsu* | 五月 |

| June | rokugatsu | 六月 |
| July | shichigatsu | 七月 |
| August | hachigatsu | 八月 |
| September | kugatsu | 九月 |
| October | juugatsu | 十月 |
| November | juuichigatsu | 十一月 |
| December | juunigatsu | 十二月 |

## Saying dates and months

### Saying the date

In general, by adding 日 (nichi) after the number you can make the date, but dates 1-10, 14, 19, 20, 24, and 29 have special readings.

Here is a full list of the dates.

### _Listen to track 170_

1st 一日 tsuitachi

2nd 二日 futsuka

3rd 三日 mikka

4th 四日 yokka

5th 五日 itsuka

6th 六日 muika

7th 七日 nanoka

8th 八日 youka

9th 九日 kokonoka

10th 十日 tooka

11th 十一日 juuichinichi

12th 十二日 juuninichi

13th 十三日 juusannichi

14th 十四日 juuyokka

15th 十五日 juugonichi

16th 十六日 juurokunichi

17th 十七日 juushichinichi

18th 十八日 juuhachinichi

19th 十九日 juukunichi

20th 二十日 hatsuka

21st 二十一日 nijuuichinichi

22nd 二十二日 nijuuninichi

23rd 二十三日 nijuusannichi

24th 二十四日 nijuuyokka

25th 二十五日 nijuugonichi

26th 二十六日 nijuurokunichi

27th 二十七日 nijuushichinichi

28th 二十八日 nijuuhachinichi

29th 二十九日 nijuukunichi

30th 三十日 sanjuunichi

31st 三十一日 sanjuuichinichi

## Examples:

### *Listen to track 171*

January 1st
一月一日
*ichigatsu tsuitachi*

February 14th
二月十四日
*nigatsu juuyokka*

March 3rd
三月三日
*sangatsu mikka*

May 5th
五月五日
*gogatsu itsuka*

July 7th
七月七日
*shichigatsu nanoka*

October 31st
十月三十一日
*juugatsu sanjuuichinichi*

December 25th
十二月二十五日
*juunigatsu nijuugonichi*

## Time expressions

### *Listen to track 172*

今 = *ima* = now
今日 = *kyou* = today
今朝 = kesa = this morning
今晩 = *konban* = tonight
今週 = *konshuu* = this week
今月 = *kongetsu* = this month
今年 = *kotoshi* = this year
明日 = *ashita* = tomorrow
明後日 = *asatte* = the day after tomorrow
来週 = *raishuu* = next week
再来週 = *saraishuu* = in two weeks

昨日 = *kinou* = yesterday
昨夜 = *sakuya* = last night
昨晩 = *sakuban*= last night
一昨日 = *ototoi* = the day before yesterday
去年 = *kyonen* = last year
一昨年 = *ototoshi* = two years ago
毎日 = *mainichi* = everyday
毎朝 = *maiasa* = every morning
毎晩 = *maiban* = every night
この間 = *kono aida* = the other day
先日 = *senjitsu* = the other day

These time expressions usually precede the subject of the sentence.

**Example:**

## *Listen to track 173*

*kinou, otousan wa osake wo nomimashita.*

昨日、お父さん　は　お酒　を　飲みました。

Yesterday, my father drank alcohol.

*raishuu, dizuniirando ni ikimasu.*

来週、ディズニーランド　に　行きます。

Next week I'm going to Disneyland.

## *Listen to tracks 174 and 175*

## Common verbs よく　使われている　動詞　*yoku tsukawareteiru doushi*

| Base verb | English |
|---|---|
| する<br>*suru* | to do |
| 来る<br>*kuru* | to come |
| 行く<br>*iku* | to go |
| ある<br>*aru* | to be |
| いる<br>*iru* | to be *for living creatures |
| 帰る<br>*kaeru* | to go home |
| 取る<br>*toru* | to take |
| 買う<br>*kau* | to buy |
| 飼う<br>*kau* | to have a pet |
| 会う<br>*au* | to meet |

| 飲む<br>*nomu* | to drink |
|---|---|
| 読む<br>*yomu* | to read |
| 泳ぐ<br>*oyogu* | to swim |
| 着る<br>*kiru* | to wear |
| 切る<br>*kiru* | to cut |
| 思う<br>*omou* | to think |
| 聞く<br>*kiku* | to listen |
| 聞こえる<br>*kikoeru* | to hear |
| 書く<br>*kaku* | to write |
| 遊ぶ<br>*asobu* | to play |
| 死ぬ<br>*shinu* | to die |
| 殺す<br>*korosu* | to kill |
| 待つ<br>*matsu* | to wait |
| 入る<br>*hairu* | to enter |
| 勝つ<br>*katsu* | to win |
| 負ける<br>*makeru* | to be defeated |
| 失くす<br>*nakusu* | to lose something |
| 分かる<br>*wakaru* | to understand |
| 見つける<br>*mitsukeru* | to find |

| 走る<br>*hashiru* | to run |
|---|---|
| 歩く<br>*aruku* | to walk |
| 知る<br>*shiru* | to know |
| 喋る<br>*shaberu* | to talk |
| 話す<br>*hanasu* | to speak |
| 言う<br>*iu* | to say |
| 食べる<br>*taberu* | to eat |
| 見る<br>*miru* | to see |
| 見える<br>*mieru* | to be able to see |
| 寝る<br>*neru* | to sleep |
| 教える<br>*oshieru* | to teach |
| 考える<br>*kangaeru* | to think |
| 出る<br>*deru* | to go out |
| 感じる<br>*kanjiru* | to feel |

# Grammar

## Verb stems

It is important to know the stem of the verb categories for conjugating verbs as they differ depending on the type of verb - **u-verb** or **ru-verb**.

### *Listen to track 176*

う    *u-verb e.g. kau*

る  *ru-verb e.g. taberu*

く *ku-verb* e.g. *kaku*

ぬ *nu-verb* e.g. *shinu*

む *mu-verb* e.g. *nomu*

**u-verb = change u to i to create the stem + *masu* or *masen* to make the verb positive or negative**

## *Listen to track 177*

e.g. *kau = kai > kaimasu* (buy) *kaimasen* (won't buy)

e.g. *kaku = kaki > kakimasu* (write) *kakimasen* (won't write)

e.g. *shinu = shini > shinimasu* (die) *shinimasen* (won't die)

e.g. *nomu = nomi > nomimasu* (drink) *nomimasen* (won't drink)

e.g. *asobu = asobi > asobimasu* (play) *asobimasen* (won't play)

**ru-verb = drop the *ru* + *masu* or *masen* to make the verb positive or negative**

## *Listen to track 178*

e.g. *taberu = tabe > tabemasu* (eat) *tabemasen* (won't eat)

e.g. *miru = mi > miru > mimasu* (see/look) *mimasen* (won't look)

e.g. *neru = ne > neru > nemasu* (sleep) *nemasen* (won't sleep)

# Verb conjugation chart

## *Listen to tracks 179 and 180*

| verb category | base verb | stem | present / future form | past form *polite | past form *short | *te* form |
|---|---|---|---|---|---|---|
| irreg | する suru | shi | します | しました | した | して |
| irreg | 来る kuru | ki | 来ます | 来ました | 来た | 来て |
| u | 行く iku | iki | 行きます | 行きました | 行った | 行って |
| u | ある aru | ari | あります | ありました | あった | あって |

| ru | いる<br>*iru* | *i* | います | いました | いた | いて |
|---|---|---|---|---|---|---|
| u | 帰る<br>*kaeru* | *kaeri* | 帰ります | 帰りました | 帰った | 帰って |
| u | 取る<br>*toru* | *tori* | 取ります | 取りました | 取った | 取って |
| u | 買う<br>*kau* | *kai* | 買います | 買いました | 買った | 買って |
| u | 飼う<br>*kau* | *kai* | 飼います | 飼いました | 飼った | 飼って |
| u | 会う<br>*au* | *ai* | 会います | 会いました | 会った | 会って |
| u | 飲む<br>*nomu* | *nomi* | 飲みます | 飲みました | 飲んだ | 飲んで |
| u | 読む<br>*yomu* | *yomi* | 読みます | 読みました | 読んだ | 読んで |
| u | 泳ぐ<br>*oyogu* | *oyogi* | 泳ぎます | 泳ぎました | 泳いだ | 泳いで |
| ru | 着る<br>*kiru* | *ki* | 着ます | 着ました | 着た | 着て |
| u | 切る<br>*kiru* | *kiri* | 切ります | 切りました | 切った | 切って |
| u | 思う<br>*omou* | *omoi* | 思います | 思いました | 思った | 思って |
| u | 聞く<br>*kiku* | *kiki* | 聞きます | 聞きました | 聞いた | 聞いて |
| ru | 聞こえる<br>*kikoeru* | *kikoe* | 聞こえます | 聞こえました | 聞こえた | 聞こえて |
| u | 書く<br>*kaku* | *kaki* | 書きます | 書きました | 書いた | 書いて |
| u | 遊ぶ<br>*asobu* | *asobi* | 遊びます | 遊びました | 遊んだ | 遊んで |
| u | 死ぬ<br>*shinu* | *shini* | 死にます | 死にました | 死んだ | 死んで |
| u | 殺す<br>*korosu* | *koroshi* | 殺します | 殺しました | 殺した | 殺して |
| u | 待つ<br>*matsu* | *machi* | 待ちます | 待ちました | 待った | 待って |

| | | | | | | |
|---|---|---|---|---|---|---|
| u | 入る<br>*hairu* | *hairi* | 入ります | 入りました | 入った | 入って |
| u | 勝つ<br>*katsu* | *kachi* | 勝ちます | 勝ちました | 勝った | 勝って |
| ru | 負ける<br>*makeru* | *make* | 負けます | 負けました | 負けた | 負けて |
| u | 失くす<br>*nakusu* | *nakushi* | 失くします | 失くしました | 失くした | 失くして |
| u | 分かる<br>*wakaru* | *wakari* | 分かります | 分かりました | 分かった | 分かって |
| ru | 見つける<br>*mitsukeru* | *mitsuke* | 見つけます | 見つけました | 見つけた | 見つけて |
| u | 走る<br>*hashiru* | *hashiri* | 走ります | 走りました | 走った | 走って |
| u | 歩く<br>*aruku* | *aruki* | 歩きます | 歩きました | 歩いた | 歩いて |
| u | 知る<br>*shiru* | *shiri* | 知ります | 知りました | 知った | 知って |
| u | 喋る<br>*shaberu* | *shaberi* | 喋ります | 喋りました | 喋った | 喋って |
| u | 話す<br>*hanasu* | *hanashi* | 話します | 話しました | 話した | 話して |
| u | 言う<br>*iu* | *ii* | 言います | 言いました | 言った | 言って |
| ru | 食べる<br>*taberu* | *tabe* | 食べます | 食べました | 食べた | 食べて |
| ru | 見る<br>*miru* | *mi* | 見ます | 見ました | 見た | 見て |
| ru | 見える<br>*mieru* | *mie* | 見えます | 見えました | 見えた | 見えて |
| ru | 寝る<br>*neru* | *ne* | 寝ます | 寝ました | 寝た | 寝て |
| ru | 教える<br>*oshieru* | *oshie* | 教えます | 教えました | 教えた | 教えて |
| ru | 考える<br>*kangaeru* | *kangae* | 考えます | 考えました | 考えた | 考えて |
| ru | 出る<br>*deru* | *de* | 出ます | 出ました | 出た | 出て |
| ru | 感じる<br>*kanjiru* | *kanji* | 感じます | 感じました | 感じた | 感じて |

# Making sentences in the past tense

## Vocabulary:

*kyou* 今日  today

*kinou* 昨日 yesterday

*shuumatsu* 週末 weekend

*renshuu suru* 練習する  to practice

*yuube* 夕べ  last night

## *Listen to track 181*

*kyou, Takuya-san wa gakkou ni ikimasen deshita.*

今日、 たくやさん  は  学校  に  行きません  でした。

Takuya didn't go to school today.

*mitsuki-san wa shukudai wo shimasen deshita*

みつきさん  は  宿題  を  しません  でした。

Mitsuki didn't do homework yesterday.

*shuumatsu ni risa-san wa paatii ni kimasen deshita.*

週末  に  リサさん  は  パーティー  に  来ません  でした。

Lisa didn't come to the party on the weekend.

*shuumatsu ni piano wo renshuu shimasen deshita.*

週末に  ピアノ  を  練習  しません  でした。

I didn't practice the piano on the weekend.

*yuube, imouto wa bangohan wo tabemasen deshita.*

夕べ、妹  は  晩御飯  を  食べません  でした。

My sister didn't eat dinner last night.

## The particle *wo*

- The particle *wo* is pronounced "oh."
- It comes before verbs and after a **direct object.**
- Verbs that indicate a **target** such as *kaeru* 帰る, *iku* 行く, *kuru* 来る, and *au* 会う  take the particle *ni* に  rather than *wo* を。

- Verbs that indicate movement towards a location **kaeru** 帰る, **iku** 行く, **kuru** 来る can take the particle **he** へ (pronounced as "eh") and is often interchangeable with the particle **ni**.

**Examples:**

**_Listen to track 182_**

*hon **wo** yomu / hon **wo** yomimasu*

本 を 読む / 本 を 読みます

read a book

*terebi **wo** miru / terebi **wo** mimasu*

テレビ を 見る / テレビ を 見ます

watch TV

*ongaku **wo** kiku / ongaku **wo** kikimasu*

音楽 を 聞く/ 音楽 を 聞きます

listen to music

*tenisu **wo** suru / tenisu **wo** shimasu*

テニス を する / テニス を します

play tennis

*baiorin **wo** hiku / baiorin **wo** hikimasu*

バイオリン を ひく / バイオリン を ひきます

play the violin

*densha **wo** oriru / densha wo orimasu*

電車 を 降りる / 電車 を 降ります

get off the train

*ie **ni** kaeru / ie **ni** kaerimasu*

家 に かえる / 家 に 帰ります

go home

*gakkou **ni** iku / gakkou **ni** ikimasu*

学校　に　行く　/学校　に　行きます

go to school

*eki **he** iku / eki **he** ikimasu*

駅　へ　行く　/駅　へ　行きます

go towards the station

*tomodachi **ni** au / tomodachi **ni** aimasu*

友達　に　会う　/友達　に　会います

meet a friend

*densha **ni** noru / densha **ni** norimasu*

電車　に　乗る　/電車　に　乗ります

get on the train

## Hiragana

# Lesson activities

## Exercise 1

Write these words from the "n" row.

1. *natsu* (summer) _____
2. *namae* (name) _____
3. *neru* (to sleep) _____
4. *netsu* (fever) _____
5. *nikki* (diary) _____

6. *ninja* _____
7. *nomu* (to drink) _____
8. *nozomu* (to hope) _____
9. *nureru* (to wet) _____
10. *nugu* (to undress) _____

## Exercise 2

Write these verbs in romaji.

1. see _____
2. read _____
3. write _____
4. drink _____
5. eat _____

6. listen _____
7. meet _____
8. sleep _____
9. do _____
10. go _____

# Sentence building

## Exercise 3

Write these sentences in English.

**Vocabulary:**

*otoko no hito* 男 の 人 man          *otoko no ko* 男 の 子 boy

*onna no hito* 女 の 人 woman          *onna no ko* 女 の 子 girl

1. (watashi wa) *hon wo yonda / yomimashita.* _____
2. *(watashi wa) terebi wo mita / mimashita.* _____
3. *Takuya-san wa ongaku wo kiita / kikimashita.* _____
4. *kinou, otousan wa tenisu wo shita / shimashita.* _____
5. *shuumatsu ni oneesan wa baiorin* wo *hiita / hikimashita.*

   _____

6. *otoko no hito wa densha* wo *orita / orimashita.* _____
7. *okaasan wa ie* ni *kaetta / kaerimashita.* _____
8. *otouto wa gakkou ni itta / ikimashita.* _____

9. *onna no ko wa eki he itta / ikimashita.* _____

10. *otoko no ko wa tomodachi ni atta / tomodachi ni aimashita.*

_____

11. *onna no hito wa densha ni notta / norimashita.* _____

## Exercise 4

Write these sentences in romaji.

## Vocabulary:

*tomodachi* 友達 friend

*eigakan* 映画館 cinema

*daigaku* 大学 university

*ni hanasu* に 話す talk to

1. I met my friends yesterday. _____
2. I went to university today. _____
3. I slept on the weekend. _____
4. Takuya did homework yesterday. _____
5. I spoke to the teacher today. _____
6. I hung out (played) with my friends on the weekend.

_____
7. I went to the cinema on the weekend. _____
8. I watched TV yesterday. _____
9. I played soccer on the weekend. _____
10. I practiced the violin today. _____

## Answer key

## Exercise 1

Write these words from the "n" row.

1. *natsu* (summer) なつ
2. *namae* (name) なまえ
3. *neru* (to sleep) ねる
4. *netsu* (fever) ねつ
5. *nikki* (diary) にっき
6. *ninja* にんじゃ
7. *nomu* (to drink) のむ
8. *nozomu* (to hope) のぞむ
9. *nureru* (to wet) ぬれる
10. *nugu* (to undress) ぬぐ

## Exercise 2

Write these verbs in romaji.

1. see _miru_
2. read _yomu_
3. write _kaku_
4. drink _nomu_
5. eat _taberu_

6. listen _kiku_
7. meet _au_
8. sleep _neru_
9. do _suru_
10. go _iku_

## Exercise 3

Write these sentences in English.

1. (_watashi wa_) _hon wo yonda / yomimashita._ <u>I read a book.</u>
2. (_watashi wa_) _terebi wo mita / mimashita._ <u>I watched TV.</u>
3. _Takuya-san wa ongaku wo kiita / kikimashita._ <u>Takuya listened to music.</u>
4. _kinou, otousan wa tenisu wo shita / shimashita._ <u>My father played tennis yesterday.</u>
5. _shuumatsu ni oneesan wa baiorin_ wo _hiita / hikimashita._ <u>My big sister played the violin on the weekend.</u>
6. _otoko no hito wa densha_ wo _orita / orimashita._ <u>The man got off the train.</u>
7. _okaasan wa ie_ ni _kaetta / kaerimashita._ <u>My mother went home.</u>
8. _otouto wa gakkou_ ni _itta / ikimashita._ <u>My little brother has gone to school.</u>
9. _onna no ko wa eki he itta / ikimashita._ <u>The girl went towards the station.</u>
10. _otoko no ko wa tomodachi ni atta / tomodachi ni aimashita._ <u>The boy met his friend(s).</u>
11. _onna no hito wa densha ni notta / norimashita._ <u>The woman got on the train.</u>

## Exercise 4

Write these sentences in romaji.

1. I met my friends yesterday. *kinou, tomodachi ni atta / aimashita.*
2. I went to university today. *kyou, daigaku ni itta / ikimashita.*
3. I slept on the weekend. *shuumatsu ni neta / nemashita.*
4. Takuya did homework yesterday. *kinou, Takuya-san wa shukudai wo shita / shimashita.*
5. I spoke to the teacher today. *kyou, sensei ni hanashita / hanashimashita.*
6. I hung out (played) with my friends on the weekend. *shuumatsu ni tomodachi to asonda / asobimashita.*
7. I went to the cinema on the weekend. *shuumatsu ni eigakan ni itta / ikimashita.*
8. I watched TV yesterday. *kinou, terebi wo mita / mimashita.*
9. I played soccer on the weekend. *shuumatsu ni sakkaa wo shita/ shimashita.*
10. I practiced the violin today. *kyou, baiorin wo renshuu shita / shimashita.*

# Lesson 13: What's the date today?

In this lesson, you will learn:

- Days, weeks, and years
- About New Year in Japan
- Nature vocabulary

## Days, weeks, and years

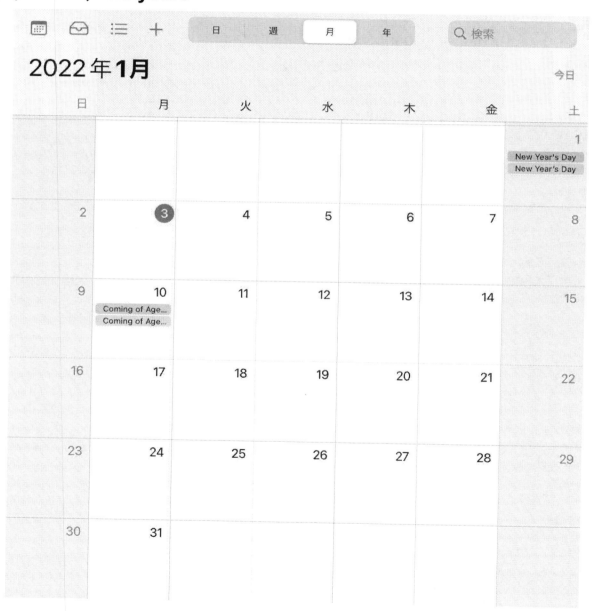

## Listen to track 183

*nichiyoubi* 日曜日 Sunday

*getsuyoubi* 月曜日 Monday

*kayoubi* 火曜日 Tuesday

*suiyoubi* 水曜日 Wednesday

*mokuyoubi* 木曜日 Thursday

*kinyoubi* 金曜日 Friday

*doyoubi* 土曜日 Saturday

## Examples:

## Listen to track 184

*nan youbi desu ka.*

何 曜日 です か。

What day is it?

*kyou wa getsuyoubi desu.*

今日 は 月曜日 です。

It's Monday today.

*ashita wa kayoubi desu.*

明日 は 火曜日 です。

It's Tuesday tomorrow.

*ashita wa nichiyoubi desu*

明日 は 日曜日 です。

It's Sunday tomorrow.

*ototoi wa doyoubi deshita.*

一昨日 は 土曜日 でした。

The day before yesterday was Saturday.

*asatte wa suiyoubi desu.*

明後日 は 水曜日 です。

It is Wednesday the day after tomorrow.

*doyoubi wa shougatsu desu.*

土曜日 は 正月 です、

It is New Year's Day on Saturday.

*getsuyoubi no asa*

月曜日 の 朝

Monday morning

*tsugi no kinyoubi*

次 の 金曜日

next Friday

*getsuyoubi kara kinyoubi made.*

月曜日 から 金曜日 まで

from Monday to Friday

*maishu kayoubi ni juku\* ni ikimasu*

毎週 火曜日 に 塾 に 行きます。

I go to cram school every Tuesday.

*\*juku* cram school

*nichiyoubi ni jinja ni ikimashita.*

日曜日 に 神社 に 行きました。

I went to a shrine on Sunday.

## More date vocabulary:

### *Listen to track 185*

今週 *(konshuu)* this week

来週 *(raishuu)* next week

先週 *(senshuu)* last week

再来週 *(saraishuu)* the week after next

今年 *(kotoshi)* this year

去年 *(kyonen)* last year

一昨年 *(ototoshi)* the year before last year

来年 *(rainen)* next year

再来年 *(sarainen)* the year after next year

閏年 *(uruudoshi)* leap year

毎年 *(maitoshi)* every year

今月 *(kongetsu)* this month

先月 *(sengetsu)* last month

先々月 *(sensengetsu)* month before last month

来月 *(raigetsu)* next month

再来月 *(saraigetsu)* next next month

毎月 *(maitsuki)* every month

毎日 *(mainichi)* every day

# Culture clip: Japan's New Year

New Year preparations start immediately on Boxing Day. There are a variety of traditional decorations that are put up after Christmas and before the 31st, but not on the 29th.

*New Year hanging decoration*

*Year of the Tiger New Year fan decoration*

Traditional dishes are eaten on New Year's Eve and New Year's Day.

## Listen to track 186

*o-sechi*: (pictured below):

*o-zouni*: a kind of hot pot soup with mochi.

*mochi*: Mochi is a sticky rice cake and can be sweet or savory. Mochi symbolizes good fortune.

*toshikoshi soba*: Soba noodles are made of buckwheat. *Toshikoshi* means "year crossing" and the long noodles symbolize longevity.

*o-sechi*

On New Year's Day and until the 3rd of January, many people go to the shrines to pull *o-mikuji* (a piece of paper like those found in Chinese fortune cookies) which has your fortune for the year written on it, pray at the shrine, and purchase *o-mamori* (an amulet with different designs such as those for passing an exam, good health, and pregnancy), *ema* (a wooden board with various designs. Traditionally people write their wishes on them and hang them in the shrine precincts), and *goshuin* stamps (a piece of paper or ink stamp to be put in a stamp book called a *goshuincho*.)

*goshuin*

*ema*

# Grammar

## Expressing the year

### *Listen to track 187*

### number + *nen* 年

2022年

*nisen nijuuni nen*

2022

2021年

*nisen nijuuichi nen*

2021

2020年

*ni sen nijuu nen*

2020

1990年

*sen kyuu hyaku kyuu juu nen*

1990

## Saying complete dates including the year

*January 3rd, 2022* is written as follows:

2022年1月3日 or 2022/01/03

## Kanji:

年 (*nen*): year

月 (*gatsu*): month

日 (*nichi*): day

With the days of the week, "Monday, January 3rd, 2022" is written as follows:

2022年1月3日 (月曜) or 2022年1月3日 (月)

The days of the week are generally written inside parentheses ( ) and placed after the day.

The day of the week is written in a short form.

Monday is 月曜日 ( *getsuyoubi*), but when it's written as part of the date, it usually becomes 月曜 (*getsuyou*) or just 月 (*getsu*).

## How to read dates in Japanese

### *Listen to track 188*

Please refer to lesson 12 for how to say the dates.

2022年1月3日 (月曜) is read as follows:

**nisennijuuni nen / ichi gatsu / mikka / getsuyou**

Literally, this is translated as:

**Two-thousand twenty-two year / one month / three day / Mon**

# Vocabulary

## *Listen to track 189*

## Nature *shizen* 自然

| English | Romaji | Kana/Kanji |
|---|---|---|
| sky | *sora* | 空 |
| sun | *taiyou* | 太陽 |
| moon | *tsuki* | 月 |
| star | *hoshi* | 星 |
| tree | *ki* | 木 |
| the Earth | *chikyuu* | 地球 |
| earth | *tsuchi* | 土 |
| fire | *hi* | 火 |
| wind | *kaze* | 風 |
| water | *mizu* | 水 |
| river | *kawa* | 川 |
| lake | *mizuumi* | 湖 |
| ocean | *umi* | 海 |
| plant | *shokubutsu* | 植物 |
| seed | *tane* | 種 |
| mountain | *yama* | 山 |
| hill | *oka* | 丘 |

# Hiragana

# Lesson activities

## Exercise 1

Write these words in hiragana using the vowels row.

1. *ari* (ant) _____
2. *arau* (to wash) _____
3. *ikutsu* (many/some) _____
4. *ima* (now) _____
5. *urayamashii* (jealous) _____
6. *ushiro* (behind) _____
7. *ebi* (shrimp) _____
8. *ehoumaki* (a thick sushi roll) _____
9. *oku* (to put) _____
10. *oriru* (to alight) _____

## Sentence building

## Exercise 2

Write these dates in kanji as shown in the examples.

1. Saturday January 1st 2022 _____
2. Friday, March 11th 2011 _____
3. Tuesday, July 7th 2020 _____
4. Sunday, October 31st 2010 _____
5. Wednesday, August 15th 1990 _____
6. Monday, May 5th 1986 _____
7. Friday, December 31st 1999 _____
8. Thursday, March 3rd 2022 _____
9. Sunday, June 19th 2022 _____
10. Monday, February 14th 2022 _____

## Exercise 3

Write these dates in English.

1. 2022年4月5日 （火） _____
2. 1995年6月9日 （金） _____
3. 2001年11月21 (水) _____

4. 2022年3月3日　(木)　_____
5. 2000年1月1日　(土)　_____
6. 2021年2月15日　(月)　_____
7. 2005年9月25日　(日)　_____
8. 2006年10月31日　(火)　_____
9. 1975年12月25日　(日)　_____
10. 1960年7月15日　(金)　_____

## Answer key

### Exercise 1

Write these words in hiragana using the vowels row.

1. *arigatou* ありがとう
2. *aru* ある
3. *ikutsu* いくつ
4. *ima* いま
5. *urayamashii* うらやましい
6. *ushiro* うしろ
7. *ebi* えび
8. *ehoumaki* えほうまき
9. *oku* おく
10. *oriru* おりる

### Exercise 2

Write these dates in kanji.

1. Saturday January 1st 2022 2022年1月1日　(土)
2. Friday, March 11th 2011 2011年3月11日　(金)
3. Tuesday, July 7th 2020 2020年7月7日　(火)
4. Sunday, October 31st 2010 2010年10月31日　(日)
5. Wednesday, August 15th 1990 1990年8月15日　(水)
6. Monday, May 5th 1986 1986年5月5日　(月)
7. Friday, December 31st 1999 1999年12月31日　(金)
8. Thursday, March 3rd 2022 2022年3月3日　(木)
9. Sunday, June 19th 2022 2022年6月19日　(日)
10. Monday, February 14th 2022 2022年2月14日　(月)

## Exercise 3

1. 2022年4月5日　(火) <u>Tuesday, April 5th 2022</u>
2. 1995年6月9日　(金) <u>Friday, June 9th 1995</u>
3. 2001年11月21 (水) <u>Wednesday, November 21st 2001</u>
4. 2022年3月3日　(木) <u>Thursday, March 3rd 2022</u>
5. 2000年1月1日　(土) <u>Saturday, January 1st 2000</u>
6. 2021年2月15日　(月) <u>Monday, February 15th 2021</u>
7. 2005年9月25日　(日) <u>Sunday, September 25th 2005</u>
8. 2006年10月31日　(火) <u>Tuesday, October 31st 2006</u>
9. 1975年12月25日　(日) <u>Sunday, December 25th 1975</u>
10. 1960年7月15日　(金) <u>Friday, July 15th 1960</u>

# Lesson 14: Asking for things

In this lesson, you will learn:

- How to say "please give me" or "please do"
- How to say "please don't do"
- The usage of the particle *ni, de*, and *he*
- Sizes vocabulary
- Locations and directions vocabulary
- More household vocabulary
- How to say "too…"

## Grammar

### Please give me (standard) / Please do / Please don't

***Listen to track 190***

~*kudasai*　ください

noun wo kudasai

*noun（名詞）を　ください*

This means "please give me…."

*kudasai* is sometimes replaced by *choudai* in casual speech.

*kudasai* may be replaced by *kure* in informal male speech.

*chokoreeto keeki wo kudasai.*

チョコレート　ケーキ　を　くださ
い。

Chocolate cake, please.

*chiizubaagaa wo kudasai.*

チーズバーガー　を　ください。

A cheeseburger, please.

*koora wo kudasai.*

コーラ　を　ください。

Cola, please.

*murasaki no wo kudasai.*

紫　の　を　ください。

The purple one, please.

***te form verb + kudasai***

**Listen to track 191**

This makes the phrase "Please do…"

The please part – *kudasai* – may also be dropped.

*kudasai* may be replaced by *kure* in informal male speech.

*paatii ni kite kudasai.*

パーティー に 来て ください。

Please come to the party.

*shukudai wo yatte kudasai.*

宿題 を やって ください。

Please do your homework.

*aisu wo tabete kudasai.*

アイス を 食べて ください。

Please eat ice cream.

*ikko totte kudasai.*

一個 取って ください。

Please take one.

*heya wo souji shite kudasai.*

部屋 を 掃除 して ください。

Please clean the room.

**verb + naide kudasai**

**Listen to track 192**

This makes the phrase "Please don't…"

The please part – *kudasai* – may also be dropped.

*kudasai* may be replaced by *kure* in informal male speech.

*shukudai wo wasurenaide.*

宿題 を 忘れないで。

Don't forget your homework.

*hitori de ikanaide kudasai.*

一人 で 行かないで ください。

Please don't go off by yourself.

*heya wo chirakasanaide.*

部屋 を 散らかさないで。

Don't mess up the room.

*Kobosanaide.*

こぼさないで。

Don't spill it.

*watashi ni hanashikakenaide kudasai.*

私 に 話しかけないで
　ください。

Please don't talk to me.

## Vocabulary:

*wasureru* 忘れる　to forget

*chirakasu* 散らかす to make a mess

*kobosu* こぼす to spill

*okoru* 怒る　to be angry

*murasaki* 紫　purple

*koora* コーラ　cola

*chokoreeto* チョコレート chocolate

*keeki* ケーキ　cake

*chiisubaagaa*　チーズバーガー cheeseburger

*souji suru* 掃除する to clean

## Please give me (polite)

### *Listen to track 193*

⌒*onegai shimasu*　お願い　します

**noun +** *wo onegai shimasu*

*Onegai shimasu* is like *kudasai*, but it can be used for something that is not a concrete object and it is considered more polite than *kudasai*.

## Examples:

*ookii no wo onegai shimasu.*

大きい の を お願いします。

A big one, please.

*kore wo onegai shimasu.*

これ を お願いします。

This one, please.

*shuuri wo onegai shimasu.*

修理　を　お願い　します。

Please repair it.

## Vocabulary:

*shuuri* 修理　repair ( *shuuri suru*　to repair)

*ashita* 明日　tomorrow

*made* まで　until/by

*ookii* 大きい　big

# The difference between に and で

に *ni*    is considered the particle of **movement.**

で *de*    is considered the particle of **action at a location**.

Compare the phrases below.

## Listen to track 194

*tomodachi to issho ni paatii **ni** ikimashita.*

友達 と 一緒に パーティー に 行きました。

I went to a party with my friends.

*paatii **de** odorimashita.*

パーティー で 踊りました。

I danced at the party.

*diizuniirando **ni** itta.*

ディズニーランド に 行った。

I went to Disneyland.

*dizuniirando **de** boushi wo katta.*

ディズニーランド で 帽子 を 買った。

I bought a hat at Disneyland.

*tomodachi ga toshokan **ni** kimashita.*

友達 が 図書館 に 来ました。

My friend came to the library.

*toshokan **de** hon wo karimashita.*

図書館 で 本 を 借りました。

I borrowed a book at the library.

に *ni* is used when saying - "I went to [place] to [purpose]."

**place (ni) object (wo) verb (ni) go/went**

## Listen to track 195

*toshokan ni hon wo kari **ni** ikimashita.*

図書館 に 本 を 借り に 行きました。

I went to the library to borrow a book.

*yuubinkyoku **ni** kitte wo kai **ni** ikimashita.*

郵便局 に 切手 を 買い に 行きました。

I went to the post office to buy a stamp.

*eigakan ni tomodachi to eiga wo mi ni itta.*

映画館 に 友達 と 映画 を 見 に 行った。

I went to the cinema to see a movie.

*kafe **ni** tomodachi ni ai **ni** itta.*

カフェ　に　友達 に 会い　に　行った。

I went to the cafe to meet my friend(s).

*the verb *au* - to meet uses the particle *ni* rather than *wo*

## The particle "e" へ

The particle へ (the kana is "*he*," but it is pronounced "eh" when being used as a particle) is used to signify movement towards somewhere. This "somewhere" is not as specific as *ni* に　where the actual destination has been decided.

### *Listen to track 196*

*harajuku **e** itte, ii resutoran wo sagashimashita.*

原宿 へ 行って、いい レストラン を 探しました。

I went towards Harajuku and looked for a nice restaurant.

*eki no hou **e** itta.*

駅 の 方 へ 行った。

I headed towards the station.

## A funny problem with particle choice

Choosing a particle can be tricky when there is a place involved.

Many speakers of Japanese as a second language mix up に、へ、and で.

Since へ has quite limited usage many people often select に.

## Too...

### *Listen to track 197*

### *sugiru*

By adding **sugimasu** to the stem of the adjective, it makes the phrase "too...".

It can be shortened to its base form **sugiru** or **sugi** in informal speech.

**Examples:**

atsusugiru

暑すぎる

too hot

kyou no tenki* wa atsusugimasu.

今日 の 天気 は 暑すぎます。

Today's weather is too hot.

*tenki 天気 weather

samusugiru

寒すぎる

too cold

nigatsu wa samusugimasu.

2月 は 寒すぎます。

February is too cold.

mabushisugiru

眩しすぎる

too bright

taiyou* wa mabushisugi.

太陽 は 眩しすぎ。

The sun is too bright.

*taiyou 太陽　sun

yosugiru

良すぎる

too good

kanojo no gijutsu* wa yosugiru.

彼女 の 技術 は 良すぎる。

Her technique is too good.

*gijutsu 技術　technique

karasugiru

辛すぎる

too spicy

kono karee* wa karasugiru.

この カレー は 辛すぎる。

This curry is too spicy.

*karee カレー curry

amasugiru

甘すぎる

too sweet

kono chokoreeto wa amasugiru.

この チョコレート は 甘すぎる。

This chocolate is too sweet.

shoppasugiru

しょっぱすぎる

too salty

otousan ga tsukuru* raamen wa shoppasugiru.

お父さん が 作る ラーメン は しょっぱすぎる。

The ramen my father makes is too salty.

*tsukuru 作る　make

*nigasugiru*

苦すぎる

too bitter

*koohii wa nigasugiru to omoimasu.*

コーヒ は 苦すぎる と 思います。

I think coffee is too bitter.

*kantansugiru*

簡単すぎる

too easy

*kono geemu wa kantansugi.*

この ゲーム は 簡単すぎ。

This game is too easy.

*muzukashisugiru*

難しすぎる

too difficult

*konshuu no shukudai wa muzukashisugimashita.*

今週 の 宿題 は 難しすぎました。

This week's homework was too difficult.

## Vocabulary

### Sizes

**Listen to track 198**

**ookii　大きい　big**

*kono shatsu wa ookii desu.*

この シャツ は 大きい です。

This shirt is big.

*ookii paakaa wo kiteimasu.*

大きい パーカー を 着ています。

I'm wearing a big hoodie.

**ookisugiru　大きすぎる　too big**

*kono pantsu wa ookisugimasu.*

この パンツ は 大きすぎます。

These underpants are too big.

**Listen to track 199**

**chiisai　ちいさい　small**

*kono hako wa chiisai desu.*

この 箱 は 小さい です。

This box is small.

*chiisai nezumi wa niwa ni imasu.*

小さい ネズミ は 庭 に います。

There's a small mouse in the garden.

**chiisasugiru**  小さすぎる  **too small**

*watashi no zubon wa chiisasugiru.*

私　の　ズボン　は　小さすぎる。

My pants are too small.

## *Listen to track 200*

**senchi**  センチ  **centimeters**

*ano buranketto wa nan senchi desu ka.*

あの　ブランケット　は　何　センチ　です　か。

How many centimeters is that blanket?

*hyaku senchi desu.*

100 センチ です。

It's 100cm.

**meetoru**  メートル  **meters**

*koko kara asoko made wa juu meetoru desu.*

ここ から あそこ まで は 10 メートル です。

It's 10 meters from here to there.

## *Listen to track 201*

## Direction & location words 方向　と　位置　*houkou to ichi*

| English | Romaji | Kanji/Kana |
|---------|--------|------------|
| on | *ue* | 上 |
| inside | *naka* | 中 |
| under | *shita* | 下 |
| next to | *tonari* | 隣 |
| by | *soba* | そば |
| in front | *mae* | 前 |
| behind | *ushiro* | 後ろ |
| straight | *massugu* | 真っ直ぐ |
| corner | *kado* | 角 |
| right | *migi* | 右 |

| | | |
|---|---|---|
| left | *hidari* | 左 |
| on the left | *hidarigawa ni aru* | 左側 に ある |
| on the right | *migigawa ni aru* | 右側 に ある |
| turn left | *hidari ni magatte* | 左 に 曲がって |
| turn right | *migi ni magatte* | 右 に 曲がって |

**_Listen to track 202_**

# Things around the house 2 家の中 2　*ie no naka 2*

| English | Romaji | Kanji/Kana |
|---|---|---|
| roof | *yane* | 屋根 |
| foyer | *genkan* | 玄関 |
| shoe storage box | *kutsubako* | 靴箱 |
| floor | *yuka* | 床 |
| bookshelf | *hondana* | 本棚 |
| carpet | *juutan* | じゅうたん |
| vacuum cleaner | *soujiki* | 掃除機 |
| iron | *airon* | アイロン |
| washing machine | *sentakki* | 洗濯機 |
| sofa | *sofa* | ソファ |
| chair | *isu* | 椅子 |
| PC | *pasokon / computer* | パソコン |
| laptop | *nooto pasokon* | ノートパソコン |
| closet | *oshire* | 押し入れ |
| chest of drawers | *tansu* | タンス |
| bedroom | *shinshitsu* | 寝室 |
| kitchen | *daidokoro / kicchin* | 台所 / キッチン |
| bathroom | *yokushitsu* | 浴室 |
| dining room | *dainingu* | ダイニング |
| toilet | *toire* | トイレ |
| living room | *ima / ribingu* | 居間　/ リビング |
| garden | *niwa* | 庭 |
| refrigerator | *reizouko* | 冷蔵庫 |
| microwave | *denshi renji* | 電子レンジ |
| garage | *shako* | 車庫 |

# Culture clip

Japanese houses have a small foyer called the **genkan** where people entering the house would remove their shoes to avoid bringing dirt into the house. Sometimes there is a box or shelf for storing shoes.

There is usually a step to go up into the main area of the house.

There are usually special toilet slippers to avoid bringing germs from the toilet floor into the rest of the house.

# Hiragana

## Compound hiragana

Compound hiragana is when smaller versions of the "y" row are combined with some kana as seen below to make a blended sound – *ryu* rather than *riyu.*

This sound can be quite challenging for non-native speakers to recognize.

| きゃ kya | きゅ kyu | きょ kyo | みゃ mya | みゅ myu | みょ myo |
|---|---|---|---|---|---|
| しゃ sya | しゅ shu | しょ sho | りゃ rya | りゅ ryu | りょ ryo |
| ちゃ cha | ちゅ chu | ちょ cho | ぎゃ gya | ぎゅ gyu | ぎょ gyo |
| にゃ nya | にゅ nyu | にょ nyo | じゃ ja | じゅ ju | じょ jo |
| ひゃ hya | ひゅ hyu | ひょ hyo | びゃ bya | びゅ byu | びょ byo |
|  |  |  | ぴゃ pya | ぴゅ pyu | ぴょ pyo |

# Listening

## _Listen to track 203_

Which do you hear, A or B?

1. a. kyuu b. kiyuu
2. a. ryuu b. riyu
3. a. shiyou. b. shou
4. a. Miyu. b. myu

5. a. kyou b kiyuu
6. a. ryou b. riyou
7. a. byouin b. biyouin
8. a. giyou b. gyou

## The correct way to write compound hiragana

The second syllable in compound hiragana should be written smaller:

**Examples:**

りゃ _rya_

きょ _kyo_

ぴゅ _pyu_

ひゃ _hya_

しょ _sho_

しゅ _shu_

# Lesson activities

## Exercise 1

Write these words that use compound hiragana.

1. *hyakuen* (100 yen)    _____
2. *shouga* (ginger)    _____
3. *shashin* (photo)    _____
4. *byouin* (hospital)    _____
5. *jagaimo* (potato)    _____
6. *gyuunyuu* (milk)    _____
7. *ryou* (amount)    _____
8. *kyuudou* (Japanese archery)    _____
9. *chouchou* (butterfly)    _____
10. *shumi* (hobby)    _____
11. *hyou* (leopard/hail)    _____
12. *gyaku* (opposite)    _____

## Sentence building

## Exercise 2

Write these phrases in English.

1. *koohi wo kudasai.*    _____
2. *ichigo keeki wo niko kudasai.*    _____
3. *akai no wo kudasai.*    _____
4. *chiisai no wo kudasai.*    _____
5. *gakkou ni kite kudasai.*    _____
6. *piano wo hiite kudasai.*    _____
7. *shukudai wo wasurenaide kudasai.*    _____
8. *hitori de ikanaide kudasai.*    _____
9. *heya wo chirakasanai kudasai.*    _____
10. *tomodachi to issho ni eigakan ni ikimashita.*    _____
11. *paatii de utaimashita.* *utau* - sing    _____
12. *USJ\* ni itta.* *USJ - Universal Studios Japan    _____
13. *USJ de tshatsu\* wo katta.* *tshatsu tシャツ – t-shirt    _____
14. *tomodachi ga watashi no ie ni kimashita.*    _____

15. *Amazon de hon wo kaimashita.* _____

16. *kono kooto\* wa ookii desu. \*kooto* コート - coat _____

17. *ano o-sara\* wa ookisugimasu. \*o-sara* お皿 - plate _____

18. *kono kappu wa chiisai* _____

19. *chiisai hamusutaa wa kago\* ni imasu. \*kago* カゴ - cage/basket

_____

20. *watashi no sukaato wa chiisasugiru.* _____

21. *gojuu senchi desu.* _____

22. *koko kara asoko made wa go meetoru desu.* _____

## Exercise 3

Write these phrases in romaji.

1.  Black tea, please. _____

2.  A cheeseburger, please. _____

3.  The blue one, please. _____

4.  The big one, please. _____

5.  Please come to my house. _____

6.  Please wash the dishes. *shokki wo arau* 食器　を　洗う - *to wash dishes*

_____

7.  Please don't go. _____

8.  Don't move. *ugoku* 動く - to move / *ugokanai* 動かない - not to move

_____

9.  I played soccer at school. _____

10. I went to Osaka. _____

11. I bought a hat at Ito Yokado. _____

12. I will go to Okinawa. _____

13. I did my homework at the library. *toshokan* 図書館 - library

_____

14. This hat is big. _____

15. These shoes are too big. _____

16. That dog is small. _____

17. My bag is too small. _____

18. It's 25cm _____

19. It's 300 meters from here to there. _____

20. I will go to America. _____

## Answer key

## Listening

Which do you hear, A or B?

1. a. kyuu **b. kiyuu**
2. **a. ryuu** b. riyu
3. **a. shiyou** b. shou
4. **a. miyu** b. myu
5. **a. kyou** b kiyuu
6. a. ryou **b. riyou**
7. **a. byouin** b. biyouin
8. a. giyou **b. gyou**

## Exercise 1

Write these words in hiragana.

1. *hyakuen* (100 yen) ひゃくえん
2. *shouga* (ginger) しょうが
3. *shashin* (photo) しゃしん
4. *byouin* (hospital) びょういん
5. *jagaimo* (potato) じゃがいも
6. *gyuunyuu* (milk) ぎゅうにゅう
7. *ryou* (amount) りょう
8. *kyuudou* (Japanese archery) きゅうどう
9. *chouchou* (butterfly) ちょうちょう
10. *shumi* (hobby) しゅみ
11. *hyou* (leopard) ひょう
12. *gyaku* (opposite) ぎゃく

## Exercise 2

Write these phrases in English.

1. *koohi wo kudasai.* Coffee, please.
2. *ichigo keeki wo niko kudasai.* Two strawberry cakes, please.
3. *akai no wo kudasai.* The red one, please.
4. *chiisai no wo kudasai.* The small one, please.
5. *gakkou ni kite kudasai.* Please come to school.
6. *piano wo hiite kudasai.* Please play the piano.
7. *shukudai wo wasurenaide kudasai.* Please don't forget your homework.
8. *hitori de ikanaide kudasai.* Don't go off by yourself.
9. *heya wo chirakasanai kudasai.* Don't mess up the room.
10. *tomodachi to issho ni eigakan ni ikimashita.* I went to the cinema with my friend.
11. *paatii de utaimashita.* I sang at the party.
12. *USJ ni itta.* I went to USJ.
13. *USJ de tshatsu wo katta.* I bought a t-shirt at USJ.

14. *tomodachi ga watashi no ie ni kimashita.* My friend(s) came to my house.

15. *Amazon de hon wo kaimashita.* I bought a book on Amazon.

16. *kono kooto wa ookii desu.* This coat is big.

17. *ano o-sara wa ookisugimasu.* That plate is too big.

18. *kono kappu wa chiisai.* That cup is small.

19. *chiisai hamusutaa wa kago ni imasu.* The small hamster is in the cage.

20. *watashi no sukaato wa chiisasugiru.* My skirt is too small.

21. *gojuusenchi desu.* It's 50 cm.

22. *koko kara asoko made wa go meetoru desu.* It's 5 meters from here to there.

## Exercise 3

Write these phrases in romaji.

1. Black tea, please. *koucha wo kudasai.*

2. A cheeseburger, please. *chiizubaagaa wo kudasai.*

3. The blue one, please. *aoi no wo kudasai.*

4. The big one, please. *ookii no wo kudasai.*

5. Please come to my house. *ie ni kite kudasai.*

6. Please wash the dishes. *shokki wo aratte kudasai.*

7. Please don't go. *ikanaide kudasai.*

8. Don't move. *ugokanaide.*

9. I played soccer at school. *gakkou de sakkaa wo shimashita.*

10. I went to Osaka. *Oosaka ni ikimashita.*

11. I bought a hat at Ito Yokado. *itoo yookadoo de boushi wo kaimashita.*

12. I will go to Okinawa. *okinawa ni ikimasu.*

13. I did my homework at the library. *toshokan de shukudai wo shimashita.*

14. This hat is big. *kono boushi wa ookii desu.*

15. These shoes are too big. *kono kutsu wa ookisugimasu.*

16. That dog is small. *ano inu wa chiisai desu.*

17. My bag is too small. *watashi no kaban wa chiisasugimasu.*

18. It's 25 cm. *niijuugo senchi desu.*

19. It's 300 meters from here to there. *koko kara asoko made wa sanbyaku meetoru desu.*

20. I will go to America. *amerika ni ikimasu.*

# Lesson 15: Because I like it

In this lesson, you will learn:

- How to count objects
- Two ways to make sentences with "because"
- Two ways to make sentences with "but"

## Grammar

### Counting objects

In **lesson 2**, we looked at the counters. Let's look at some more objects we can count with these words and practice using them in the exercises below.

### The most useful counters

The most important two to remember are 一つ (Kun reading number + **tsu**) and 一個 (commonly used reading number + **ko**).

### Example:

#### Listen to track 204

*banana sheeki hitotsu*

バナナ シェーキ 一つ

one banana milkshake

*koora futatsu*

コーラ 二つ

two colas

*koohi mitsu*

コーヒー 三つ

three coffees

*mikan ikko*

みかん 一個

one mandarin

*nikuman niko*

肉まん 二個

two pork buns

*kurowassan sanko*

クロワッサン 三個

three croissants

### Counters that you should be able to recognize

Some of these have some tricky readings, so watch out!

## _Listen to track 205_

## 本 (hon/bon/pon) counter for long and thin items

_sooseeji ippon_ ソーセージ　いっぽん one sausage

_enpitsu nihon_ えんぴつ　にほん　 two pencils

_pen sanbon_ ぺん　さんぼん three pens

_sooseeji yonhon_ ソーセージ　よんほん four sausages

_enpitsu gohon_ えんぴつ　ごほん　 five pencils

_pen roppon_ ぺん　ろっぽん six pens

_sooseeji nanahon_ ソーセージ　ななほん seven sausages

_enpitsu happon_ えんぴつ　はっぽん　 eight pencils

_pen kyuuhon_ ぺん　きゅうほん nine pens

_sooseeji juppon_ ソーセージ　じゅっぽん　 ten sausages

## Exercise 1

Write these phrases in romaji using the vocabulary to assist you.

_fude_ 筆　 _brush_

_jougi_ 定規　 ruler

_mushimegane_ 虫メガネ magnifying glass

_fooku_ フォーク fork

_hari_ 針 needle

_hashi_ 箸　 chopsticks

1. two chopsticks　　　_____
2. three rulers　　　_____
3. four needles　　　_____
4. five forks　　　_____
5. six brushes　　　_____
6. seven magnifying glasses _____

### Listen to track 206

## 枚 (mai) counter for flat items

*kami ichimai* かみ　いちまい one piece of paper

*kaado nimai* カード　にまい　two cards

*CD sanmai* シーディー　さんまい　three CDs

*kami yonmai* かみ　よんまい four pieces of paper

*kaado gomai* カード　ごまい　five cards

*CD rokumai* シーディー　ろくまい　six CDs

*kami nanamai* かみ　ななまい seven pieces of paper

*kaado hachimai* カード　はちまい　eight cards

*CD kyuumai* シーディー　きゅうまい　nine CDs

*kami juumai* かみ　じゅうまい　ten pieces of paper

## Exercise 2

Write these phrases in romaji using the vocabulary to assist you.

*shatsu* シャツ shirt

*chokoreeto* チョコレート chocolate

*chiketto* チケット ticket

*piza* ピザ pizza

*kitte* 切手 ticket

*shashin* 写真 photo

*pan* パン　bread

1. seven pieces of chocolate _____
2. eight shirts _____
3. nine photos _____
4. ten pizzas _____
5. six slices of bread _____
6. one stamp _____

## *Listen to track 207*

## 匹 (hiki/biki/piki) counter for animals

*neko ippiki* ネコ　いっぴき one cat

*inu nihiki* いぬ　にひき two dogs

*hamusutaa sanbiki* ハムスター　さんびき three hamsters

*neko yonhiki* ネコ　よんひき four cats

*inu gohiki* いぬ　ごひき two dogs

*hamusutaa roppiki* ハムスター　ろっぴき six hamsters

*neko nanahiki* ネコ　ななひき seven cats

*inu happiki* いぬ　はっぴき two dogs

*hamusutaa kyuuhiki* ハムスター　きゅうひき nine hamsters

*neko juppiki* ネコ　じゅっぴき ten cats

## Exercise 3

Write these phrases in romaji using the vocabulary to assist you.

*shika* 鹿 deer

*nezumi* ネズミ mouse

*ookami* 狼　wolf

*sakana* 魚 fish

*suzumebachi* スズメバチ hornet

*ari* アリ ant

1.  a hundred hornets _____
2.  ten deer _____
3.  fifty fish _____
4.  twenty wolves _____
5.  a thousand ants _____
6.  five hundred mice _____

## Listen to track 208

**頭 (tou) counter for large animals, rare animals, working animals, and animals in facilities**

*zou ittou* ぞう　いっとう one elephant

*chinpanjii nitou* チンパンジー　にとう two chimpanzees

*gorira santou* ゴリラ　さんとう three gorillas

*saru yontou* サル　よんとう four monkeys

*panda gotou* パンダ　ごとう　five pandas

*hitsuji rokutou* ひつじ　ろくとう six sheep

*buta nanatou* ぶた　ななとう seven pigs

*ushi hattou* うし　はっとう eight cows

*ookami kyuutou* おおかみ　きゅうとう nine wolves

*inu juttou*　いぬ　じゅっとう ten dogs

## Exercise 4

Write these phrases in romaji using the vocabulary to assist you.

*tora* トラ tiger

*panda* パンダ　panda

*yagi* ヤギ　goat

*sai* サイ rhino

*uma* 馬　horse

1. seven tigers _____
2. one panda _____
3. three goats _____
4. ten horses _____
5. two rhinos _____

## <u>Listen to track 209</u>

## 羽 (wa) counter for birds, bats, and rabbits

*usagi ichiwa* ウサギ　いちわ　one rabbit

*usagi niwa* ウサギ　にわ two rabbits

*usagi sanwa* ウサギ　さんわ three rabbits

*usagi yonwa* ウサギ　よんわ four rabbits

*usagi gowa* ウサギ　ごわ five rabbits

*tori rokuwa* とり　ろくわ six birds

*tori nanawa* とリ　ななわ　seven birds

*koumori hachiwa* コウモリ　はちわ eight bats

*koumori kyuuwa* コウモリ　きゅうわ nine bats

*koumori juuwa* コウモリ　じゅうわ ten bats

## Exercise 5

*taka* 鷹 hawk

*fukurou* フクロウ owl

*hato* 鳩 pigeon

*usagi* ウサギ rabbit

*koumori* コウモリ bat

Write these phrases in English using the vocabulary to assist you.

1. *usagi ichiwa*　_____
2. *koumori niwa*　_____
3. *hato sanwa*　_____
4. *fukurou yonwa*　_____
5. *taka gowa*　_____

## *Listen to track 210*

## 冊 (satsu) counter for books

*hon issatsu* ほん　いっさつ　one book

*hon nisatsu* ほん　にさつ two books

*hon sansatsu* ほん　さんさつ three books

*hon yonsatsu* ほん　よんさつ four books

*hon gosatsu* ほん　ごさつ five books

*hon rokusatsu* ほん　ろくさつ six books

*hon nanasatsu* ほん　ななさつ seven books

*hon hassatsu* ほん　はっさつ eight books

*hon kyuusatsu* ほん　きゅうさつ nine books

*hon juusatsu* ほん　じゅうさつ ten books

## Exercise 6

Write these phrases in English.

1. *hon rokusatsu* _____
2. *hon juusatsu* _____
3. *hon hassatsu* _____
4. *hon nanasatsu* _____
5. *hon kyuusatsu* _____

## *Listen to track 211*

## 台 (dai) counter for vehicles, furniture, electronics, large instruments, and whole cakes

*kuruma ichidai* くるま　いちだい one car

*torakku nidai* トラック　にだい two trucks

*hondana sandai* ほんだな　さんだい three bookshelves

*keeki yondai* ケーキ　よんだい four whole cakes

*baiku godai* バイク　ごだい five motorcycles

*piano rokudai* ピアノ　ろくだい six pianos

*doramu nanadai* ドラム　ななだい seven drum sets

*kurumaisu hachidai* くるまいす　はちだい eight wheelchairs

*kuruma kyuudai* くるま　きゅうだい nine cars

*kuruma juudai* くるま　じゅうだい ten cars

## Exercise 7

Write these phrases in English using the vocabulary to assist you.

*kurumaisu* 車椅子 wheelchair

*jitensha* 自転車　bicycle

*heri* ヘリ helicopter

*tansu* タンス chest of drawers

*kuruma* くるま car

1. *kurumaisu ichidai* _____
2. *heri nidai* _____
3. *tansu sandai* _____
4. *kuruma yondai* _____
5. *jitensha godai* _____

## Listen to track 212

## 分 (fun/pun) counter for minutes

*ippun* いっぷん　1 minute

*nifun* にふん　2 minutes

*sanpun* さんぷん　3 minutes

*yonpun* よんぷん　4 minutes

*gofun* ごふん　5 minutes

*roppun* ろっぷん　6 minutes

*nanafun* ななふん　7 minutes

*happun* はっぷん　8 minutes

*kyuufun* きゅうふん　9 minutes

*juppun* じゅっぷん 10 minutes

## Exercise 8

Write these times in romaji.

1. five minutes _____
2. three minutes _____
3. ten minutes _____

4. four minutes _____

5. one minute _____

## Listen to track 213

## 年 (nen) years

*ichinen* いちねん 1 year

*ninen* にねん 2 years

*sannen* さんねん 3 years

*yonnen* よねん 4 years

*gonen* ごねん 5 years

*rokunen* ろくねん 6 years

*nananen* ななねん 7 years

*hachinen* はちねん 8 years

*kyuunen* きゅうねん 9 years

*juunen* じゅうねん 10 years

## Exercise 9

Write these phrases in English.

1. *hachinen* _____

2. *ninen* _____

3. *yonnen* _____

4. *sannen* _____

5. *nananen* _____

## Listen to track 214

## 日 (nichi/ka) counter for days

Note that one is pronounced as (*tsuitachi* ついたち) for "**the first of**" when talking about the days of the month rather than the number of days.

*ichinichi* いちにち 1 day

*futsuka* ふつか 2 days

*mikka* みっか 3 days

*yokka* よっか 4 days

*itsuka* いつか 5 days

*muika* むいか 6 days

*nanoka* なのか 7 days

*youka* ようか 8 days

*kokonoka* ここのか 9 days

*tooka* とおか 10 days

## Exercise 10

Write these phrases in English.

1. *tooka* _____
2. *itsuka* _____
3. *ichinichi* _____
4. *nanoka* _____
5. *yokka* _____

## Listen to track 215

## 人 (nin) counter for people

There are some special readings for certain numbers as shown below.

*hitori* ひとり one person

*futari* ふたり two people

*sannin* さんにん three people

*yonin* よにん four people

*gonin* ごにん five people

*rokunin* ろくにん six people

*nananin* ななにん seven people

*hachinin* はちにん eight people

*kyuunin* きゅうにん nine people

*juunin* じゅうにん ten people

## Exercise 11

Write these phrases in English.

1. *hitori* _____
2. *nananin* _____
3. *futari* _____
4. *kyuunin* _____
5. *yonin* _____

## Listen to track 216

## ケ月 (kagetsu) counter for months

ikkagetsu いっかけつ one month

nikagetsu にかげつ two months

sankagetsu さんかげつ three months

yonkagetsu よんかげつ four months

gokagetsu ごかげつ five months

rokkagetsu ろっかげつ six months

nanakagetsu ななかげつ seven months

hakkagetsu はっかげつ eight months

kyuukagetsu きゅうかげつ nine months

jukkagetsu じゅっかげつ ten months

## Exercise 12

Write these months in romaji.

1. six months _____
2. twelve months _____
3. one month _____
4. three months _____
5. seven months _____

## *Listen to track 217*

### 時 (ji) o'clock

*ichiji* いちじ　1 o'clock

*niji* にじ 2 o'clock

*sanji* さんじ 3 o'clock

*yoji* よじ 4 o'clock

*goji* ごじ 5 o'clock

*rokuji* ろくじ 6 o'clock

*shichiji* しちじ 7 o'clock

*hachiji* はちじ 8 o'clock

*kuji* くじ 9 o'clock

*juuji* じゅうじ 10 o'clock

*juuichiji* じゅういちじ 11 o'clock

*juuniji* じゅうにじ 12 o'clock

## Exercise 13

Write these times in English.

1. *juuji* _____
2. *sanji* _____
3. *shichiji* _____
4. *kuji* _____
5. *juuniji* _____

## *Listen to track 218*

### 時間 (jikan) counter for hours

*ichijikan* いちじかん　1 hour

*nijikan* にじかん　2 hours

*sanjikan* さんじかん 3 hours

*yojikan* よじかん　4 hours

*gojikan* ごじかん 5 hours

*rokujikan* ろくじかん 6 hours

*nanajikan* ななじかん 7 hours

*hachijikan* はちじかん 8 hours

*kujikan* くじかん 9 hours

*juujikan* じゅうじかん 10 hours

## Exercise 14

Write these times in romaji.

1. 24 hours _____
2. 8 hours _____
3. 5 hours _____
4. 1 hour _____
5. 4 hours _____

## *Listen to track 219*

### 回 (kai) counter for occurrences

*ikkai*   いっかい once

*nikai*   にかい twice

*sankai* さんかい   three times

*yonkai* よんかい   four times

*gokai*   ごかい five times

*rokkai*   ろっかい six times

*nanakai*   ななかい seven times

*hakkai / hachikai* はっかい・ はちかい   eight times

*kyuukai* きゅうかい nine times

*jukkai* じゅっかい ten times

## Exercise 15

Write these phrases in romaji.

1. seven times _____
2. once _____
3. five times _____
4. ten times _____
5. eight times _____

## *Listen to track 220*

## 階  (kai/gai) counter for floors

*ikkai*   いっかい   first floor

*nikai*   にかい  second floor

*sangai / sankai* さんがい/さんかい  third floor

*yonkai* よんかい   fourth floor

*gokai*   ごかい  fifth floor

*rokkai*   ろっかい  sixth floor

*nanakai*   ななかい  seventh floor

*hakkai / hachikai* はっかい ・ はちかい  eighth floor

*kyuukai* きゅうかい  ninth floor

*jukkai* じゅっかい  tenth floor

## Exercise 16

Write these phrases in romaji.

    1.  fourth floor  _____

    2.  first floor  _____

    3.  six floor  _____

    4.  tenth floor  _____

    5.  third floor  _____

## *Listen to track 221*

## 歳/才   (sai) counter for ages

*issai* いっさい 1 years old

*nisai*   にさい 2 years old

*sansai*   さんさい 3 years old

*yonsai* よんさい   4 years old

*gosai* ごさい 5 years old

*rokusai* ろくさい 6 years old

*nanasai* ななさい 7 years old

*hassai* はっさい eight years old

*kyuusai* きゅうさい nine years old

*jussai* じゅっさい ten years old

*for twenty years old, a special reading – *hatachi* はたち – is used.

## Exercise 17

Write these ages in English.

1.  *jussai* _____
2.  *issai* _____
3.  *gosai* _____
4.  *yonjuunisai* _____
5.  *hachijuunana* _____
6.  *nanajuusansai* _____
7.  *nijuunisai* _____
8.  *kyuujuuyonsai* _____
9.  *hyakusai* _____
10. *juurokusai* _____

## The counters and particles

The particle "*no*" can also be used to express the number of something.

Be aware of the word order.

Compare the sentences below:

### *Listen to track 222*

### Sentence pattern 1

*neko nihiki*

猫　2匹

2 cats

### Sentence pattern 2

*nihiki no neko*

2匹　の　猫

2 cats

### Saying "but"

### *Listen to track 223*

が　*ga*

*ga* is the most polite way to say "**but**".

**Examples:**

*sumimasen ga, sore wa watashi no desu.*

すみません が、それ は 私 の です。

Excuse me, but that is mine.

*ikimashita ga, daremo imasen deshita.*

行きましたが、誰も いません でした。

I went, but nobody was there.

## Listen to track 224

でも *demo*

*demo* comes at the start of the sentence and has a more informal sound to it.

*sasottekurete arigatou. demo, shukudai ga takusan aru kara ikenai\* n da.*

誘ってくれて ありがとう。でも、宿題 が たくさん ある から 行けない ん だ。

Thanks for inviting me. But I have a lot of homework, so I can't go.

\* *ikemasen* 行けません can't go

## Listen to track 225

しかし *shikashi*

*shikashi* has quite a formal sound to it and comes at the start of the sentence.
It is often translated as "*however.*"

*shikashi, raishuu wa ikemasu.*

しかし、来週 は 行けます。

However, I can go next week.

# Saying "because"

### Listen to track 226

## から *kara*

*kara* is a common way to say "**because**".

It can precede a verb.

*shukudai ga takusan aru kara ikenai n da.*

宿題　が　たくさん　ある　から　行けない　ん　だ。

I have a lot of homework, so I can't go.

*onaka ga itakatta kara desu.*

お腹　が　痛かった　から　です。

It was because I had a stomach ache.

### Listen to track 227

## ので *node*

*node* is another way to say "**because**."

*node* sounds more formal than *kara*.

Note: When "**node**" follows a noun or adjective the particle *na* is used.

*byouki na node, shigoto ni ikemasen.*

病気 な ので、仕事 に 行けません。

I am sick, so I cannot go to work.

*takusan shukudai ga aru node, paatii ni ikemasen.*

たくさん　宿題　が　ある　ので、パーティー に 行けません。

I have a lot of homework, so I can't go to the party.

*itsumo\* renshuu suru\* node, piano ga jouzu ni narimashita.*

いつも 練習 する ので、ピアノ が 上手 に なりました。

I have gotten better at playing the piano, because I always practice.

\**itsumo* いつも　always

\**renshuu suru* 練習　する to practice

# Vocabulary

## *Listen to track 228*

**At school** 学校 で　**gakkou de**

| English | Romaji | Kanji/Kana |
|---|---|---|
| desk | *tsukue* | 机 |
| classroom | *kyoushitsu* | 教室 |
| teacher | *sensei / kyoushi* | 先生　・　教師 |
| student | *seito / gakusei* | 生徒・ 学生 |
| blackboard | *kokuban* | 黒板 |
| whiteboard | *howaito boodo* | ホワイトボード |
| textbook | *kyoukasho* | 教科書 |
| book | *hon* | 本 |
| cafeteria | *shokudou* | 食堂 |
| library | *toshokan* | 図書館 |
| nurse's office | *hokenshitsu* | 保健室 |
| music room | *ongaku kyoushitsu* | 音楽教室 |
| arts & crafts room | *zukou kyoushitsu* | 図工 教室 |
| pencil | *enpitsu* | 鉛筆 |
| pen | *pen* | ペン |
| ruler | *jougi* | 定規 |
| pencil case | *fudebako / pen keesu* | 筆箱　・ ペンケース |
| chalk | *chooku* | チョーク |
| eraser | *keshigomu* | 消しゴム |
| playground | *guraundo* | グラウンド |
| school uniform | *seifuku* | 制服 |
| randoseru backpack | *randoseru* | ランドセル |
| marker | *maakaa* | マーカー |
| crayon | *kureyon* | クレヨン |
| colored pencils | *iroenpitsu* | 色鉛筆 |
| paint | *penki / enogu* | ペンキ・ 絵の具 |
| paper | *kami* | 紙 |
| notebook | *nooto* | ノート |
| elementary school | *shougakkou* | 小学校 |
| junior high school | *chuugakkou* | 中学校 |
| high school | *koukou* | 高校 |
| university | *daigaku* | 大学 |

## *Listen to track 229*

## At the office 職場 で   shokuba de

| English | Romaji | Kanji/Kana |
|---|---|---|
| PC | *pasokon* | パソコン |
| laptop | *nooto pasokon* | ノートパソコン |
| computer | *konpyuutaa* | コンピューター |
| company | *kaisha* | 会社 |
| office | *jimusho* | 事務所 |
| phone | *denwa* | 電話 |
| email | *iimeeru* | eメール |
| text message | *meeru* | メール |
| cell phone | *keitai denwa* | 携帯電話 |
| smart phone | *sumaho* | スマホ |
| money | *okane* | お金 |
| overtime | *zangyou* | 残業 |
| customer/guest | *o-kyakusan / o-kyakusama* | お客さん ・ お客様 |
| correction tape | *shuusei teepu* | 修正テープ |
| printer | *purintaa* | プリンター |
| fax machine | *fakusuki* | FAX機 |
| employee | *juugyouin* | 従業員 |
| staff | *sutaffu* | スタッフ |
| hole puncher | *anaake panchi* | 穴あけ パンチ |
| highlighter | *keikou pen* | 蛍光 ペン |
| company president | *shachou* | 社長 |
| general manager | *buchou* | 部長 |
| section manager | *kachou* | 課長 |
| Immediate boss | *joushi* | 上司 |
| secretary | *hisho* | 秘書 |

## *Listen to track 230*

## Insects 虫   *mushi*

| English | Romaji | Kanji/Kana |
|---|---|---|
| spider | *kumo* | 蜘蛛 |
| bee | *hachi* | 蜂 |
| fly | *hae* | ハエ |

| caterpillar | *aomushi* | 青虫 |
|---|---|---|
| moth | *ga* | 蛾 |
| butterfly | *chouchou* | 蝶々 |
| worm | *mimizu* | ミミズ |
| beetle | *kabutomushi* | 甲虫 |
| cricket | *koorogi* | コオロギ |
| cockroach | *gokiburi* | ゴキブリ |
| praying mantis | *kamakiri* | カマキリ |
| hornet | *suzumebachi* | 雀蜂 |
| centipede | *mukade* | ムカデ |

# Hiragana

## Exercise 18

Write these common words in hiragana.

1.  *yasai* (vegetables) _____
2.  *yuki* (snow) _____
3.  *yoroshiku* (Please get along with me.) _____
4.  *rainichi* (coming to Japan) _____
5.  *ringo* (apple) _____
6.  *rui* (type) _____
7.  *rekishi* (history) _____
8.  *roujin* (elderly person) _____
9.  *watashi* (I/me) _____
10. *gin* (silver) _____
11. *mamire* (covered with…) _____
12. *mushi* (bug/ignore) _____
13. *mezasu* (to aim) _____
14. *mori* (forest) _____
15. *hazure* (to miss) _____
16. *hikouki* (airplane) _____

# Lesson activities

## Sentence building

### Exercise 19

### Vocabulary:

*tanoshii* 楽しい　fun

*nemashita* 寝ました　slept

Write these phrases in English.

1. *onaka ga itakatta kara, nemashita* _____
2. *tanoshii kara desu.* _____
3. *tanoshii node, suki desu.* _____

### Exercise 20

Write these phrases in romaji.

### Vocabulary:

*atama ga itai* 頭　が　痛い　headache

*oishii* 美味しい　delicious

1. I can't go because my head hurts. _____
2. I can't go, because I have a lot of homework. _____
3. I like cake, because it's delicious. _____

## Answer key

### Exercise 1

Write these phrases in romaji using the vocabulary to assist you.

1. two chopsticks *hashi nihon / nihon no o-hashi*
2. three rulers *jougi sanbon / sanbon no jougi*
3. four needles *hari yonhon / yonhon no hari*
4. five forks *fooku gohon / gohon no fooku*
5. six brushes *fude roppon / roppon no fude*
6. seven magnifying glass *mushimegane nanahon / nanahon no mushimegane*

## Exercise 2

Write these phrases in romaji using the vocabulary to assist you.

1. seven pieces of chocolate _chokoreeto nanamai_
2. eight shirts _shatsu hachimai_
3. nine photos _shashin kyuumai_
4. ten pizzas _piza juumai_
5. six slices of bread _pan rokumai_
6. one stamp _kitte ichimai_

## Exercise 3

Write these phrases in romaji using the vocabulary to assist you.

1. a hundred hornets _suzumebachi hyappiki_
2. ten deer _shika juppiki_
3. fifty fish _sakana gojuppiki_
4. twenty wolves _ookami nijuppiki_
5. a thousand ants _ari senbiki_
6. five hundred mice _nezumi gohyappiki_

## Exercise 4

Write these phrases in romaji using the vocabulary to assist you.

1. seven tigers _tora nanatou_
2. one panda _panda ittou_
3. three goats _yagi santou_
4. ten horses _uma juttou_
5. two rhinos _sai nittou_

## Exercise 5

Write these phrases in English using the vocabulary to assist you.

1. _usagi ichiwa_ one rabbit
2. _koumori niwa_ two bats
3. _hato sanwa_ three pigeons
4. _fukurou yonwa_ four owls
5. _taka gowa_ five hawks

## Exercise 6

Write these phrases in English.

1. _hon rokusatsu_ six books
2. _hon juusatsu_ ten books
3. _hon hassatsu_ eight books
4. _hon nanasatsu_ seven books
5. _hon kyuusatsu_ nine books

## Exercise 7

Write these phrases in English using the vocabulary to assist you.

1. *kurumaisu ichidai* <u>one wheelchair</u>
2. *heri nidai* <u>two helicopters</u>
3. *tansu sandai* <u>three chest of drawers</u>
4. *kuruma yondai* <u>four cars</u>
5. *jitensha godai* <u>five bicycles</u>

## Exercise 8

Write these times in romaji.

1. five minutes *<u>gofun</u>*
2. three minutes *<u>sanpun</u>*
3. ten minutes *<u>juppun</u>*
4. four minutes *<u>yonpun</u>*
5. one minute *<u>ippun</u>*

## Exercise 9

Write these phrases in English.

1. *hachinen* <u>eight years</u>
2. *ninen* <u>two years</u>
3. *yonnen* <u>four years</u>
4. *sannen* <u>three years</u>
5. *nananen* <u>seven years</u>

## Exercise 10

Write these phrases in English.

1. *tooka* <u>ten days</u>
2. *itsuka* <u>five days</u>
3. *ichinichi* <u>one day</u>
4. *nanoka* <u>seven days</u>
5. *yokka* <u>four days</u>

## Exercise 11

Write these phrases in English.

1. *hitori* <u>one person</u>
2. *nananin* <u>seven people</u>
3. *futari* <u>two people</u>
4. *kyuunin* <u>nine people</u>
5. *yonin* <u>four people</u>

## Exercise 12

Write these months in romaji.

1. six months *rokkagetsu*
2. twelve months *juunikagetsu*
3. one month *ikkagetsu*
4. three months *sankagetsu*
5. seven months *nanakagetsu*

## Exercise 13

Write these times in English.

1. *juuji* ten o'clock
2. *sanji* three o'clock
3. *shichiji* seven o'clock
4. *kuji* nine o'clock
5. *juuniji* ten o'clock

## Exercise 14

Write these times in romaji.

1. 24 hours *nijuuyo jikan*
2. 8 hours *hachi jikan*
3. 5 hours *go jikan*
4. 1 hour *ichi jikan*
5. 4 hours *yo jikan*

## Exercise 15

Write these phrases in romaji.

1. seven times *nanakai*
2. once *ikkai*
3. five times *gokai*
4. ten times *jukkai*
5. eight times *hakkai*

## Exercise 16

Write these phrases in romaji.

1. fourth floor *yonkai*
2. first floor *ikkai*
3. six floor *rokkai*
4. tenth floor *jukkai*
5. third floor *sangai*

## Exercise 17

Write these ages in English.

1. *jussai* <u>ten years old</u>
2. *issai* <u>one year old</u>
3. *gosai* <u>five years old</u>
4. *yonjuunisai* <u>forty- two years old</u>
5. *hachijuunana* <u>eighty-seven years old</u>
6. *nanajuusansai* <u>seventy-three years old</u>
7. *nijuunisai* <u>twenty-two years old</u>
8. *kyuujuuyonsai* <u>ninety-four years old</u>
9. *hyakusai* <u>one hundred years old</u>
10. *juurokusai* <u>sixteen years old</u>

## Exercise 18

Write these common words in hiragana.

1. *yasai* (vegetables) <u>やさい</u>
2. *yuki* (snow) <u>ゆき</u>
3. *yoroshiku* (Please get along with me) <u>よろしく</u>
4. *rainichi* (coming to Japan) <u>らいにち</u>
5. *ringo* (apple) <u>りんご</u>
6. *rui* (type) <u>るい</u>
7. *rekishi* (history) <u>れきし</u>
8. *roujin* (elderly person) <u>ろうじん</u>
9. *watashi* (I/me) <u>わたし</u>
10. *gin* (silver) <u>ぎん</u>
11. *mamire* (covered with…) <u>まみれ</u>
12. *mushi* (bug/ignore) <u>むし</u>
13. *mezasu* (to aim) <u>めざす</u>
14. *mori* (forest) <u>もり</u>
15. *hazure* (to miss) <u>はずれ</u>
16. *hikouki* (airplane) <u>ひこうき</u>

## Exercise 19

Write these phrases in English.

1. *onaka ga itakatta kara, nemashita.* <u>My stomach was hurting, so I slept.</u>
2. *tanoshii kara desu.* <u>Because it's fun.</u>
3. *tanoshii node, suki desu.* <u>It's fun, so I like it.</u>

## Exercise 20

Write these phrases in romaji.

1. I can't go because my head hurts.
   <u>*atama ga itai kara, ikenai / ikemasen.*</u>
   <u>*atama ga itai node, ikenai / ikemasen*</u>

2. I can't go because I have a lot of homework.
   <u>*shukudai ga takusan aru kara, ikenai / ikemasen.*</u>
   <u>*shukudai ga takusan aru node, ikenai / ikemasen.*</u>

3. I like cake because it's delicious.
   <u>*keeki wa oishii kara, suki (desu).*</u>
   <u>*keeki wa oishii node, suki (desu).*</u>

# Lesson 16: Let's do it

In this lesson, you will learn:

- Making negative forms
- Frequency adverbs
- Making the *te* form
- Making the *teiru* form
- More about time particles
- Nationalities vocabulary
- Languages vocabulary

## Grammar

In this section, we will look at more ways of conjugating verbs. Please refer to lesson 12 for the conjugation chart.

### Making polite negatives

*polite present negative: ru-verb stem + masen*

#### Listen to track 231

tabemasu   > tabemasen

食べます   > 食べません

eat          > don't eat

mimasu > mimasen

見ます  > 見ません

see     > don't see

nemasu > nemasen

寝ます   > 寝ません

sleep     > don't sleep

### polite present negative - u-verb stem + masen

### Listen to track 232

*kaimasu > kaimasen*

買います > 買いません

buy > don't buy

*machimasu > machimasen*

待ちます > 待ちません

wait > don't wait

*ikimasu > ikimasen*

行きます > 行きません

go > don't go

*hanashimasu > hanashimasen*

話します > 話しません

talk > don't talk

*yomimasu > yomimasen*

読みます > 読みません

read > don't read

*shinimasu > shinimasen*

死にます > 死にません

die > don't die

## Polite past negative

### *ru*-verb stem + *masen deshita*

### Listen to track 233

*tabemasen > tabemasen deshita*

食べません > 食べません　でした

don't eat > didn't eat

*mimasen > mimasen deshita*

見ません > 見ません　でした

don't look > didn't look

*nemasen > nemasen deshita*

寝ません > 寝ません　でした

slept > didn't sleep

### *u*-verb stem + *masen deshita*

### Listen to track 234

*kaimasen > kaimasen deshita*

買いません > 買いません　でした

don't buy > didn't buy

*machimasen > machimasen deshita*

待ちません > 待ちません　でした

don't wait > didn't wait

ikimasen        > ikimasen deshita

行きません  > 行きません　でした

don't go        > didn't go

shinimasen > shinimasen deshita

死にません　死にません　でした

don't die     > didn't die

hanashimasen > hanashimasen deshita

話しません      >話しません　でした

don't talk       > didn't talk

oyogimasen > oyogimasen deshita

泳ぎません　泳ぎません　でした

don't swim    > didn't swim

yomimasen   > yomimasen deshita

読みません  >読みません　でした

don't read      > didn't read

## Negative short form

### ru-verb stem + nai

### Listen to track 235

Short affirmative > short negative

taberu     > tabenai

食べる    > 食べない

eat           > don't eat

neru   > nenai

寝る   > 寝ない

sleep  > don't sleep

miru     > minai

見る     > 見ない

see       > don't see

### u-verb negative stem + nai

When making the short form, change the final kana to the "a" row and add nai.

### Listen to track 236

kau > kawanai

買う　買わない

buy  > don't buy

matsu > matanai

待つ　待たない

wait    > don't wait

iku > ikanai

行く　行かない

go > don't go

hanasu > hanasanai

話す　話さない

talk　> don't talk

yomu > yomanai

読む　読まない

read　> don't read

shinu > shinanai

死ぬ　死なない

die　> don't die

oyogu > oyoganai

泳ぐ　> 泳がない

swim　> didn't swim

## Negative past short form

### ru-verb stem + nakatta

### Listen to track 237

tabenai　> tabenakatta

食べない　> 食べなかった

don't eat　> didn't eat

### u-verb negative stem + nakatta

When making the short form, change the final kana to the "**a**" row and add nakatta.

### Listen to track 238

kawanai > kawanakatta

買わない > 買わなかった

don't buy > didn't buy

matanai > matanakatta

待たない > 待たなかった

don't wait > didn't wait

ikanai　> ikanakatta

行かない > 行かなかった

don't go　> didn't go

hanasanai > hanasanakatta

話さない　> 話さなかった

don't talk　> didn't talk

*yomanai* > *yomanakatta*

読まない > 読まなかった

don't read > didn't read

*oyoganai* > *oyoganakatta*

泳がない > 泳がなかった

don't swim > didn't swim

*shinanai* > *shinanakatta*

死なない > 死ななかった

don't die > didn't die

## Negative conjugation chart

### Listen to track 239 and 240

| Verb category | Base verb | *Stem* | Negative *polite | Negative *short | Past negative *polite | Past negative *short |
|---|---|---|---|---|---|---|
| irreg | する suru | shi | しません | しない | しませんでした | しなかった |
| irreg | 来る kuru | ki | 来ません | 来ない ! konai | 来ませんでした | 来なかった |
| u | 行く iku | iki | 行きません | 行かない | 行きました | 行かなかった |
| u | ある aru | ari | ありません | ない | ありませんでした | なかった |
| ru | いる iru | i | いません | いない | いませんでした | いた |
| u | 帰る kaeru | kaeri | 帰りません | 帰らない | 帰りませんでした | 帰った |
| u | 取る toru | tori | 取りません | 取らない | 取りませんでした | 取った |
| u | 買う kau | kai | 買いません | 買わない | 買いました | 買った |
| u | 飼う kau | kai | 飼いません | 飼わない | 飼いました | 飼った |
| u | 会う au | ai | 会いません | 会わない | 会いました | 会った |
| u | 飲む nomu | nomi | 飲みません | 飲まない | 飲みました | 飲んだ |

| u | 読む<br>*yomu* | *yomi* | 読みません | 読まない | 読みました | 読んだ |
|---|---|---|---|---|---|---|
| u | 泳ぐ<br>*oyogu* | *oyogi* | 泳ぎません | 泳がない | 泳ぎました | 泳いだ |
| ru | 着る<br>*kiru* | *ki* | 着ません | 着ない | 着ました | 着た |
| u | 切る<br>*kiru* | *kiri* | 切りません | 切らない | 切ました | 切った |
| u | 思う<br>*omou* | *omoi* | 思いません | 思わない | 思いました | 思った |
| u | 聞く<br>*kiku* | *kiki* | 聞きません | 聞かない | 聞きました | 聞いた |
| ru | 聞こえる<br>*kikoeru* | *kikoe* | 聞こえません | 聞こえない | 聞こえました | 聞こえた |
| u | 書く<br>*kaku* | *kaki* | 書きません | 書かない | 書きました | 書いた |
| u | 遊ぶ<br>*asobu* | *asobi* | 遊びません | 遊ばない | 遊びました | 遊んだ |
| u | 死ぬ<br>*shinu* | *shini* | 死にません | 死なない | 死にました | 死んだ |
| u | 殺す<br>*korosu* | *koroshi* | 殺しません | 殺さない | 殺しました | 殺した |
| u | 待つ<br>*matsu* | *machi* | 待ちません | 待たない | 待ちました | 待った |
| u | 入る<br>*hairu* | *hairi* | 入りません | 入らない | 入りました | 入った |
| u | 勝つ<br>*katsu* | *kachi* | 勝ちません | 勝たない | 勝ちました | 勝った |
| ru | 負ける<br>*makeru* | *make* | 負けません | 負けない | 負けました | 負けた |
| u | 失くす<br>*nakusu* | *nakushi* | 失くしません | 失くさない | 失くしました | 失くした |
| u | 分かる<br>*wakaru* | *wakari* | 分かりません | 分からない | 分かりました | 分かった |
| ru | 見つける<br>*mitsukeru* | *mitsuke* | 見つけません | 見つけない | 見つけました | 見つけた |
| u | 走る<br>*hashiru* | *hashiri* | 走りません | 走らない | 走りました | 走った |

| u | 歩く<br>*aruku* | *aruki* | 歩きませ<br>ん | 歩かない | 歩きました | 歩いた |
| u | 知る<br>*shiru* | *shiri* | 知りませ<br>ん | 知らない | 知りました | 知った |
| u | 喋る<br>*shaberu* | *shaberi* | 喋りませ<br>ん | 喋らない | 喋りました | 喋った |
| u | 話す<br>*hanasu* | *hanashi* | 話しませ<br>ん | 話さない | 話しました | 話した |
| u | 言う<br>*iu* | *ii* | 言いませ<br>ん | 言わない | 言いました | 言った |
| ru | 食べる<br>*taberu* | *tabe* | 食べませ<br>ん | 食べない | 食べました | 食べた |
| ru | 見る<br>*miru* | *mi* | 見ません | 見ない | 見ました | 見た |
| ru | 見える<br>*mieru* | *mie* | 見えませ<br>ん | 見えない | 見えました | 見えた |
| ru | 寝る<br>*neru* | *ne* | 寝ません | 寝ない | 寝ました | 寝た |
| ru | 教える<br>*oshieru* | *oshie* | 教えませ<br>ん | 教えない | 教えました | 教えた |
| ru | 考える<br>*kangaeru* | *kangae* | 考えませ<br>ん | 考えない | 考えました | 考えた |
| ru | 出る<br>*deru* | *de* | 出ません | 出ない | 出ました | 出た |
| ru | 感じる<br>*kanjiru* | *kanji* | 感じませ<br>ん | 感じない | 感じました | 感じた |
| false ru | 走る<br>*hashiru* | *hashiri* | 走りませ<br>ん | 走らない | 走りました | 走った |

## Polite versus informal speaking

As you may have seen throughout this book, polite forms have **desu** at the end of the sentence or **verb stem~masu.**

So, the polite form is often called the **desu/masu form**.

Informal speech is usually reserved for good friends and family and should be avoided when speaking to someone who is senior to you or to a customer.

# Conjugating verbs into the polite form

## Affirmative polite form

To create the affirmative polite form, take the **verb stem** (refer to the chart above) and add *masu*.

### Listen to track 241

*taberu > tabemasu*

食べる > 食べます

eat

*kau > kaimasu*

買う > 買います

buy

*iku > ikimasu*

行く > 行きます

go

*kuru > kimasu*

来る > 来ます

come

*hanasu > hanashimasu*

話す　 > 話します

speak

*shinu > shinimasu*

死ぬ　 > 死にます

die

*yomu > yomimasu*

読む > 読みます

read

*oyogu > oyogimasu*

泳ぐ　 > 泳ぎます

swim

## Sentence building

### Subject + object + verb

### Listen to track 242

*watashi wa niku wo tabemasu.*

私 は 肉 を 食べます。

I eat meat.

*watashi wa geemu wo kaimashita.*

私 は ゲーム を 買いました。

I bought a game.

*watashi wa gakkou ni ikimasen deshita.*

私 は 学校 に 行きません でした。

I didn't go to school.

*tomodachi wa paatii ni kimashita.*

友達 は パーティー に 来ました

My friend came to the party.

sensei to hanashimashita.

先生　と　話しました。

I spoke with the teacher.

teki wa shinimashita.

敵　は　死にました。

The enemy died.

otousan wa shinbun wo yomimasu.

お父さん　は　新聞　を　読みます。

My father reads the newspaper.

## Frequency adverbs

### Listen to track 243

itsumo いつも　always

taitei たいてい　usually

tokidoki ときどき　sometimes

mettani 〜verb+nai めったに〜verb+ない / mettani ~masen めったに〜verb+ません rarely

watashi wa **yoku** koora wo nomimasu.

私　は　よく　コーラ　を　飲みます。

I often drink cola.

watashi wa **mettani** geemu wo kai**masen.**

私　は　めったに　ゲーム　を　買いません。

I rarely buy games.

watashi wa **itsumo** shukudai wo shimasu.

私　は　いつも　宿題　を　します。

I always do my homework.

tomodachi wa **tokidoki** uchi ni kimasu.

友達　は　ときどき　家　に　来ます。

My friends sometimes come to my home.

sensei wa **taitei** shukudai wo dashimasu.

先生　は　たいてい　宿題　を　出します。

My teacher usually gives homework.

*shuumatsu ni kare wa **tokidoki** puuru ni ikimasu.*

週末　に　彼　は　ときどき　プール　に　行きます。

On the weekend, he sometimes goes to the pool.

*shuumatsu ni otousan wa **itsumo** terebi wo mimasu.*

週末　に　お父さん　は　いつも　テレビ　を　見ます。

On the weekend, my father always watches TV.

## The *te* form

The *te* form is used to make the polite requests in a shortened form, but it is also necessary for creating the *teiru* form that will also be covered in this lesson.

### *ru*-verbs

### <u>Listen to track 244</u>

*miru   > mite*

見る　　>見て

look   > please look

*taberu    > tabete*

食べる　>食べて

eat        > please eat

*neru   > nete*

sleep  > please sleep

寝る　　>寝て

### *u*-verb ending

*u*-verbs can be categorized based on their final kana.

These are important to know when making the *te* form and *te-iru* form.

### *Tsu, u* & false *ru*-verbs

### *u/tsu/ru > tte*

## Listen to track 245

kau > katte

買う　>買って

buy > please buy

toru　> totte

取る　>取って

take > please take

matsu > matte

待つ　>待って

wait > please wait

## mu, nu & gu-verb ending

## gu > de

## Listen to track 246

oyogu > oyoideiru (oyoideimasu)

泳ぐ　>泳いでいる　(泳いでいます)

swim　> swimming

## mu > de

yomu　> yondeiru (yondeimasu)

読む　>読んでいる　(読んでいます)

read　> reading

## nu > de

shinu　> shindeiru (shindeimasu)

死ぬ　>死んでいる　(死んでいます)

die　　> dying

## su-verb ending

## su > shite

## *Listen to track 247*

*hanasu > hanashiteiru (hanashiteimasu)*

話す　　＞話している　（話しています）

speak　＞ speaking

### *ku*-verb ending

### ku > ite

*kiku > kiite*

聞く　　　　＞聞いて

*listen/ask > please listen/ask*

*one exception: *iku > itte*

## The *teiru* form

The **teiru** form expresses the same meaning as -**ing** in English.

### *ru*-verbs

## *Listen to track 248*

*miru > miteiru (miteimasu)*

見る＞見ている　（見ています）

look > looking

*taberu > tabeteiru (tabeteimasu)*

食べる＞食べている　（食べています）

eat > eating

*neru > neteiru (neteimasu)*

寝る＞寝ている　（寝ています）

sleep > sleeping

### *u*-verb ending

*U*-verbs can be categorized based on their final kana.

These are important to know when making the *te* form and *te-iru* form.

### tsu, u &62 > tteiru

Listen to track 249

kau    > katteiru (katteimasu)

買う   >買っている　(買っています)

buy    > buying

toru   > totteiru (totteimasu)

取る   >取っている　(取っています)

take   > taking

matsu > matteiru (matteimasu)

待つ　>待っている　(待っています)

wait　> waiting

## Mu, nu & gu-verb ending

Listen to track 250

### gu > deiru

oyogu > oyoideiru (oyoideimasu)

泳ぐ　>泳いでいる　(泳いでいます)

swim > swimming

### mu > deiru

yomu > yondeiru (yondeimasu)

読む　>読んでいる　(読んでいます)

read > reading

### nu > deiru

shinu > shindeiru (shindeimasu)

死ぬ　>死んでいる　(死んでいます)

die > dying

### su-verb ending

## Listen to track 251

### su > shiteiru

hanasu > hanashiteiru (hanashiteimasu)

話す　＞話している　（話しています）

speak　＞speaking

### ku-verb ending

kiku　　＞kiiteiru (kiiteimasu)

聞く　　＞聞いている　（聞いています）

listen/ask ＞ listening/asking

*one exception: iku > itte (itteimasu)

## Location particles に　and へ

に is used to express motion to a specific location.

## Listen to track 252

watashi wa toshokan ni ikimasu.

私　は　図書館　に　行きます。

I'm going to the library.

kare wa paatii ni kimashita

彼　は　パーティー　に　来ました。

He came to the party.

imouto wa eigakan ni ikimashita.

妹　は　映画館　に　行きました。

My little sister went to the cinema.

## Time particle に

Time particle ni is used with years, months, days of the week, and clock time.

**ni** is **not** used with 今日 kyou, 明日　ashita, 昨日　kinou, 朝　asa, 晩　ban, いつ itsu, 今〜　kon〜, 来〜rai〜。

## Examples:

## Listen to track 253

2023 ni sotsugyou* shimashita.

2023年　に　卒業　しました。

I graduated in 2023.

*sotsugyou suru 卒業　する to graduate

1990 ni imouto ga umaremashita.*
1990年　に　妹　が　生まれました。
My sister was born in 1990.

*umareru 生まれる to be born

kugatsu ni kekkon shimasu.*
九月　に　結婚　します。
I will get married in September.

*kekkon suru 結婚　する　to get married

hachigatsu ni shiken* ga arimasu.
8月　に　試験　が　あります。
I have an exam in August.

*shiken 試験 exam

shuumatsu ni ryokou* ni ikimasu.
週末　に　旅行　に　行きます。
I'm going on a trip on the weekend.

*ryokou 旅行　trip / 旅行　する ryokou suru to travel

getsuyoubi ni gakkou ni ikimasu.
月曜日　に　学校に　行きます。
I go to school on Mondays.

nichiyoubi ni ibento ni ikimasu.
日曜日　に　イベント　に　行きます。
I'm going to an event on Sunday.

kuji ni ongaku no jugyou ga arimasu.
9時　に　音楽　の　授業　が　あります。

I have music class at 9 o'clock.

*rokuji ni bangohan wo tabemasu.*

6時　に　晩御飯　を　食べます。

I eat dinner at 6 o'clock.

## Sentence structure using verbs

### *Listen to track 254*

### The basic Japanese sentence order

subject は　object を　verb

*watashi **wa** terebi **wo** mimasu.*

私　は　テレビ　を　見ます。

I watch TV.

### Complex sentence:

Subject は time reference に　place　で　person と　object を　verb

*watashi **wa** juuji **ni** eigakan **de** tomodachi **to** eiga **wo** mimasu.*

私　は　10時　に　映画館　で　友達　と　映画　を　見ます。

I am going to watch a movie at the cinema with my friend(s).

### Using the verb *suru* する

*suru* on its own means "to do."

The polite form of *suru* is *shimasu*.

*suru* is often paired with nouns to create verbs.

### *Listen to track 255*

*renshuu* 練習　= practice (noun)

*renshuu suru* 練習　する　= to practice (verb)

The verb *asobu* 遊ぶ　means "to play," but *suru* is used with sports to means "to play [a sport]."

### Examples:

*watashi wa tenisu wo shimasu.*

私　は　テニス　を　します。

I play tennis.

*otouto wa basukettobooru wo shimasu.*

弟　は　バスケットボール　を　します。

My little brother plays basketball.

*otousan wa yakkyuu wo shimasu.*

お父さん　は　野球　を　します。

My father plays baseball.

# Vocabulary

## *Listen to track 256*

## Languages 言語　*gengo*

| English | Romaji | Kana/Kanji |
|---|---|---|
| English | *eigo* | 英語 |
| Japanese | *nihongo* | 日本語 |
| Korean | *kankokugo* | 韓国語 |
| Chinese | *chuugokugo* | 中国語 |
| Arabic | *arabiago* | アラビア語 |
| Italian | *itariago* | イタリア語 |
| French | *furansugo* | フランス語 |
| German | *doitsugo* | ドイツ語 |
| Spanish | *supeingo* | スペイン語 |
| Portuguese | *porutogarugo* | ポルトガル語 |
| Russian | *roshiago* | ロシア語 |
| Thai | *taigo* | タイ語 |

## *Listen to track 257*

## Nationalities 国籍 *kokuseki*

| English | Romaji | Kana/Kanji |
|---|---|---|
| American | *amerikajin* | アメリカ人 |
| British | *igirisujin* | イギリス人 |
| Canadian | *kanadajin* | カナダ人 |
| Australian | *oosutorariajin* | オーストラリア人 |
| Japanese | *nihonjin* | 日本人 |
| Korean | *kankokujin* | 韓国人 |
| Chinese | *chuugokujin* | 中国人 |
| Arabian | *arabiajin* | アラビア人 |
| Italian | *itariajin* | イタリア人 |
| French | *fransujin* | フランス人 |
| German | *doitsujin* | ドイツ人 |
| Spanish | *supeinjin* | スペイン人 |
| Portuguese | *porutogarujin* | ポルトガル |
| Russian | *roshiajin* | ロシア人 |
| Thai | *taijin* | タイ人 |

# Lesson activities

## Sentence building

### Exercise 1

Write these verbs in English.

1. *iku* _____
2. *suru* _____
3. *neru* _____
4. *matsu* _____
5. *kiku* _____
6. *kakanai* _____
7. *yomanai* _____
8. *konai* _____
9. *shinanai* _____
10. *omoimasen deshita* _____
11. *kangaemasen deshita* _____
12. *nakushimasen deshita* _____
13. *shirimasen deshita.* _____
14. *wakarimasen* _____
15. *mimasen* _____
16. *kikimasen* _____
17. *arimasen* _____

### Exercise 2

1. didn't go _____
2. didn't come _____
3. didn't sleep _____
4. didn't read _____
5. didn't drink _____
6. don't know _____
7. don't do _____
8. don't walk _____
9. don't run _____
10. think _____
11. speak _____
12. eat _____

## Exercise 3

Write these phrases in English.

1. *kinou, watashi wa basukettobooru wo shita.*
   _____

2. *oniisan wa kouen de yakkyuu wo shi ni itta.*
   _____

3. *imouto wa tenisu wo shimasu.*
   _____

4. *shuumatsu ni otousan wa bareebooru wo shimashita.*
   _____

5. *kinyoubi ni gakkou ni ikimashita.*
   _____

## Answer key

## Sentence building

## Exercise 1

Write these verbs in English.

1. *iku* <u>go</u>
2. *suru* <u>do</u>
3. *neru* <u>sleep</u>
4. *matsu* <u>wait</u>
5. *kiku* <u>listen</u>
6. *kakanai* <u>don't write</u>
7. *yomanai* <u>don't read</u>
8. *konai* <u>don't come</u>
9. *shinanai* <u>don't die</u>
10. *omoimasen deshita* <u>didn't think</u>
11. *kangaemasen deshita* <u>didn't think</u>
12. *nakushimasen deshita* <u>didn't lose</u>
13. *shirimasen deshita.* <u>didn't know</u>
14. *wakarimasen* <u>don't know/understand</u>
15. *miemasen* <u>don't look</u>

16. *kikimasen* <u>don't listen</u>
17. *arimasen* <u>don't have / there isn't</u>

## Exercise 2

1. didn't go *ikanakatta / ikimasen deshita*
2. didn't come *konakatta / kimasen deshita*
3. didn't sleep *nenakatta / nemasen deshita*
4. didn't read *yomanakatta / yomimasen deshita*
5. didn't drink *nomanakatta / nomimasen deshita*
6. don't know *wakaranai / wakarimasen*
7. don't do *shinai / shimasen*
8. don't walk *arukanai / arukimasen*
9. don't run *hashiranai / hashirimasen*
10. think *kangaeru / kangaemasu / omou / omoimasu*
11. speak *hanasu / hanashimasu*
12. eat *taberu / tabemasu*

## Exercise 3

Write these phrases in English.

1. *kinou, watashi wa basukettobooru wo shita.* <u>I played basketball yesterday.</u>
2. *oniisan wa kouen de yakkyuu wo shi ni itta.* <u>My big brother went to the park to play baseball.</u>
3. *imouto wa tenisu wo shimasu* <u>My little sister plays tennis.</u>
4. *shuumatsu ni otousan wa bareebooru wo shimashita.* <u>My father played volleyball on the weekend.</u>
5. *kinyoubi ni gakkou ni ikimashita.* <u>I went to school on Friday.</u>

# Lesson 17: I went there at 12:30

In this lesson, you will learn:

- How to tell time
- Putting time into sentences in the future
- Putting time into sentences in the past
- More time related particles

## Grammar

### Telling time

To say "o'clock," add the kanji for "hour" - *ji* - after the *onyomi* number.

*Listen to track 258*

***ima nanji desu ka?***

今　何時　です　か。

What time is it?

| | | | |
|---|---|---|---|
| 12:00 | 12時 | *juuniji* | |
| 1:00 | 1時 | *ichiji* | |
| 2:00 | 2時 | *niji* | |
| 3:00 | 3時 | *sanji* | |
| 4:00 | 4時 | *yoji* | |
| 5:00 | 5時 | *goji* | |

6:00　6時　*rokuji*

7:00　7時　*shichiji*

8:00　8時　*hachiji*

9:00　9時　*kuji*

10:00　10時　*juuji*

11:00　11時　*juuichiji*

**Examples**:

### Talking about routines

*Listen to track 259*

*hachiji ni okimasu.*

8時　に　起きます。

I wake up at 8 o'clock.

*kuji ji piano wo renshuu shimasu.*

9時　に　ピアノ　を　練習　します。

I play the piano at 9 o'clock.

*juuji ni bentou wo tsukurimasu.*

10時　に　弁当　を　作ります

I make a lunch box at 10 o'clock.

## Talking about plans

The present simple form can also be used to express the future or plans, but you can be more specific about it being a "scheduled action" by adding **yotei** after the **base form of the verb.**

### *Listen to track 260*

*juuichiji ni shigoto ni iku yotei desu.*

11時　に　仕事　に　行く予定です。

I plan to leave for work at 11 o'clock.

*juuniji ni densha ni noru yotei desu.*

12時　に　電車　に　乗る予定です。

I plan to get on the train at 12 o'clock.

*ichiji ni kaigi ni shusseki suru yotei desu.*

1時　に　会議　に　出席　する　予定　です。

I plan to participate in a meeting at 1 o'clock.

## Talking about completed activities

### *Listen to track 261*

*ichiji ni hirugohan wo tabemashita.*

1時　に　昼ごはん　を　食べました。

I ate lunch at 1 o'clock.

*juuji ni kaerimashita.*

10時　に　帰りました。

I went home at 10 o'clock.

*juuniji ni nemashita.*

12時　に　寝ました。

I went to sleep at 12 o'clock.

## Dialogue

### _Listen to track 262_

_Takuya: okaasan, ima nanji?_

たくや: お母さん、今 何時?

Takuya: Mom, what time is it?

_okaasan: rokuji. hayaku okinasai._

お母さん: 6時。早く 起きなさい。

Mother: It's 6 o'clock. Hurry up and get up.

_Takuya: wakatta._

たくや: 分かった。

Takuya: Okay.

_Mitsuki: sensei, ima nanji desu ka._

みつき: 先生、今 何時 ですか。

Mitsuki: Teacher, what time is it?

_sensei: ichiji desu. jugyou ga hajimarimasu._

先生: 1時です。授業 が 始まります。

Teacher: It's 1 o'clock. Class is going to start.

_Mitsuki: sensei, shukudai wo wasuremashita._

みつき: 先生、宿題 を 忘れました。

Mitsuki: Teacher, I forgot my homework.

_sensei: mata desu ka._

先生 : また です か。

Teacher: Again?

## AM and PM

To make a time AM, add 午前 (**_gozen_**) before the time.

### *Listen to track 263*

| | | | |
|---|---|---|---|
| 12:00am 午前12時 *gozen juuniji* | | 6:00am 午前6時 *gozen rokuji* | |
| 1:00am 午前1時 *gozen ichiji* | | 7:00am 午前7時 *gozen shichiji* | |
| 2:00am 午前2時 *gozen niji* | | 8:00am 午前8時 *gozen hachiji* | |
| 3:00am 午前3時 *gozen sanji* | | 9:00am 午前9時 *gozen kuji* | |
| 4:00am 午前4時 *gozen yoji* | | 10:00am 午前10時 *gozen juuji* | |
| 5:00am 午前5時 *gozen goji* | | 11:00am 午前11時 *gozen juuichiji* | |

## Examples:

### *Listen to track 264*

*gozen rokuji ni okita.*

午前 6時 に 起きた。

I woke up at 6am.

*gozen shichiji ni asagohan wo tabeta.*

午前 7時に 朝ご飯 を 食べた。

I ate breakfast at 7am.

*gozen hachiji ni undou shita.*

午前 8時に 運動 した。

I exercised at 8am.

*gozen kuji ni heya wo souji shita.*

午前 9時 に 部屋 を 掃除 した。

I cleaned my room at 9am.

*gozen juuji ni nihongo wo benkyou suru yotei.*

午前 10時 に 日本語 を 勉強 する 予定。

I plan to study Japanese at 10am.

*gozen juuichiji ni inu wo sanpo wo suru yotei.*

午前 11時 に 犬 の 散歩 を する 予定。

I plan to walk the dog at 11am.

To make a time PM, add 午後 (*gogo*) before the time.

**_Listen to track 265_**

12:00pm 午後12時   *gogo juuniji*

1:00pm   午後1時 *gogo ichiji*

2:00pm   午後2時 *gogo niji*

3:00pm   午後3時 *gogo sanji*

4:00pm   午後4時 *gogo yoji*

5:00pm   午後5時 *gogo goji*

6:00pm   午後6時 *gogo rokuji*

7:00pm   午後7時 *gogo shichiji*

8:00pm   午後8時 *gogo hachiji*

9:00pm   午後9時 *gogo kuji*

10:00pm   午後10時 *gogo juuji*

11:00pm   午後11時 *gogo juuichiji*

**Examples:**

**_Listen to track 266_**

*gogo ichiji ni geemu wo shimasu.*

午後 1時   に   ゲーム   を   します。

I play games at 1pm.

*gogo niji ni sentaku wo shimashita.*

午後 2時   に   洗濯   を   しました。

I did the laundry at 2pm.

*gogo sanji ni shokki wo arau yotei desu.*

午後 3時   に   食器   を   洗う   予定   です。

I plan to wash the dishes at 3pm.

*gogo yoji ni onrain jugyou wo shimashita.*

午後 4時   に   オンライン   授業   を   しました。

I had an online class at 4pm.

*gogo goji ni shukudai wo shimasu.*

午後 5時   に   宿題   を   します。

I do my homework at 5pm.

*gogo rokuji ni bangohan wo tabemasu.*

午後 6時   に   晩御飯   を   食べます。

I eat dinner at 6pm.

*gogo shichiji ni terebi wo mimasu.*

午後 7時 に テレビ を 見ます。

I watch TV at 7pm.

*gogo hachiji ni hon wo yomimasu.*

午後 8時 に 本 を 読みます。

I read books at 8pm.

*gogo kuji ni sakkaa wo shimashita.*

午後 9時 に サッカー を しました。

I played soccer at 9pm.

*gogo juuji ni oyatsu wo tabemashita.*

午後 10時 に おやつ を 食べました。

I ate snacks at 10pm.

*gogo juuichiji ni ofuro ni hairu yotei desu.*

午後 11時 に お風呂 に 入る 予定 です。

I plan to have a bath at 11pm.

## Half past

To say "half past," add 半 **(han)** after the time.

### Listen to track 267

12:30 12時半  *juuniji han*

1:30  1時半 *ichiji han*

2:30  2時半 *niji han*

3:30  3時半 *sanji han*

4:30  4時半 *yoji han*

5:30  5時半 *goji han*

6:30  6時半 *rokuji han*

7:30  7時半 *shichiji han*

8:30  8時半 *hachiji han*

9:30  9時半 *kuji han*

10:30  10時半 *juuji han*

11:30  11時半 *juuichiji han*

## Examples:

### *Listen to track 268*

*gozen kujihan ni shawaa wo abita.*

午前 9時半 に シャワー を 浴びた。

I took a shower at 9:30am.

*gozen juujihan ni basu ni noru yotei.*

午前 10時半 に バス に 乗る 予定。

I plan to get on the bus at 10:30am.

*gozen juuichijihan ni suupaa ni iku yotei desu.*

午前 11時半 に スーパー に 行く予定　です。

I plan to go to the supermarket at 11:30am.

*gogo ichijihan ni tomodachi to asobimasu.*

午後 1時半 に 友達 と 遊びます。

I hang out with my friends at 1pm.

*gogo nijihan ni ryouri wo shita.*

午後 2時半 に 料理 を した

I cooked at 2:30pm

*gogo sanjihan ni kaigi ni iku yotei desu.*

午後 3時半 に 会議 に　行く　予定　です。

I plan to go to a meeting at 3:30pm.

*gogo yoji han ni jimu ni ikimasu.*

午後 4時半 に ジム に 行きます。

I go to the gym at 4:30pm.

*gogo gojihan ni deeto ni iku yotei.*

午後 5時半 に デート に 行く　予定。

I have a date at 5:30pm.

*gogo rokujihan ni o-sake wo nonda.*

午後 6時半　に　お酒　を　飲んだ。

I drank alcohol at 6:30pm.

## Dialogue:

*Listen to track 269*

*Takuya: Risa-san, shuumatsu wa hima desu ka.*

たくや: リサさん、週末 は 暇 です か。

Takuya: Lisa, are you free this weekend?

*Risa: doyoubi no gozen juuji ni akihabara ni iku yotei desu.*

リサ: 土曜日 の 午前 10時 に 秋葉原 に 行く 予定 です。

Lisa: I'm going to Akihabara at 10am on Saturday.

*Takuya: gogo hachiji ni eiga wo mi ni ikimasen ka.*

たくや: 午後 8時 に 映画 を 見 に 行きません か。

Takuya: Would you like to see a movie with me at 8pm?

*Risa: ii desu ne.*

リサ: いい です ね。

Lisa: That sounds nice.

*Takuya: yatta!*

たくや: やった！

Takuya: Yay!

# Listening

Listen to the dialogue and answer the questions.

*Listen to track 270*

## Vocabulary:

*yuuenchi* 遊園地　amusement park

*juku* 塾　cram school (Many Japanese children go to a cram school for extra lessons after school.)

1. What time is Lisa going to cram school?
2. What time does Takuya suggest for the date?
3. What time will they go to the amusement park?

## Culture clip

To avoid rudely refusing an invitation or request, you can use the word **chotto.** It actually means "a little," but it can be used to suggest that you can't or don't want to do something without directly refusing.

**Examples:**

### *Listen to track 271*

*sore wo tsukatte mo ii desu ka?*

それ　を　使って　も　いい　です　か。

Can I use that?

*nn, sore wa chotto.*

んん、それ　は　ちょっと。

Mm, I'd rather you didn't.

*ashita, asobi ni ikou.*

明日、遊び　に　行こう

Let's go and hang out tomorrow.

*gomen, ashita wa chotto.*

ごめん、明日　は　ちょっと。

Sorry, tomorrow is not so good for me.

## Using the particle *gurai* ぐらい　and *goro* ごろ

### *Listen to track 272*

Both **goro**（ごろ) and **gurai**（ぐらい）are used to express approximation.

The difference, however, is that 頃　**goro** is only used for a **specific point in time**, while **gurai** is used with a duration.

## Examples:

*sanjuppun gurai kakaru.*

30分 ぐらい かかる。

It will take around 30 minutes.

*rokuji goro ni hajimarimasu.*

6時　ごろ　に　始まります。

It will start at around 10 o'clock.

*koko kara byouin made go kiro gurai desu.*

ここ から 病院 まで 5キロ ぐらい です。

It is about 5 kilometers to the hospital from here.

*futsuka goro*

2日 ごろ

around the 2nd (of the month)

*futsuka gurai*

2日 ぐらい

around 2 days

# Lesson activities

## Sentence building

### Exercise 1

Write these times in romaji.

1. 3:00pm _____
2. 10:00am _____
3. 8:00am _____
4. 2:00pm _____
5. 7:00am _____

6. 1:00pm _____
7. 9:00am _____
8. 11:00am _____
9. 12:00pm _____
10. 4:00pm _____

### Exercise 2

Write these times using kanji (refer to lesson 2 for numbers).

1. 10:00pm _____
2. 5:00am _____
3. 7:00am _____
4. 6:00pm _____
5. 11:00am _____

6. 2:00pm _____
7. 10:00am _____
8. 6:00am _____
9. 12:00pm _____
10. 8:00pm _____

### Exercise 3

Write these times in English.

1. *gozen ichiji* _____
2. *gogo hachiji* _____
3. *gozen yoji* _____
4. *gozen rokuji* _____
5. *gogo niji* _____

6. *gogo yoji* _____
7. *gogo goji* _____
8. *gogo kuji* _____
9. *gozen shichiji* _____
10. *gozen juuichiji* _____

### Exercise 4

Write these sentences in romaji.

1. I wake up at 7:30am.
2. I play the guitar at 8:30pm.
3. I make a lunch box at 9am.
4. I go to work at 9:30am.
5. I get on the train at 10am.

_____
_____
_____
_____
_____

6. I eat lunch at 1:30pm.  _____
7. I go home at 7:30pm.  _____
8. I go to sleep at 10:30pm.  _____

## Exercise 5

Write these sentences in English.

1. *gozen gojihan ni okimasu.*  _____
2. *gozen rokujihan ni asagohan wo tabemasu.*  _____
3. *gozen kuji ni nihongo wo benkyou shimasu.*  _____
4. *gozen shichiji ni undou shimasu.*  _____
5. *gozen hachiji ni shigoto ni ikimasu.*  _____
6. *gozen hachijihan ni densha ni norimasu.*  _____
7. *gogo sanji ni hirugohan wo tabemasu.*  _____
8. *gogo shichijihan ni kaerimasu.*  _____
9. *gogo hachijihan ni bangohan wo tabemasu.*  _____
10. *gozen niji ni nemasu.*  _____

## Answer key

## Listening answers and script

Listen to the dialogue and answer the questions.

## Vocabulary:

*yuuenchi* 遊園地  amusement park

*juku* 塾 cram school

1. What time is Lisa going to cram school? <u>9am</u>
2. What time does Takuya suggest for the date? <u>12pm</u>
3. What time will they go to the amusement park? <u>2pm</u>

*Takuya: Risa-san, shuumatsu wa hima desu ka.*

たくや: リサさん、週末 は 暇 です か。

Takuya: Lisa, are you free this weekend?

*Risa: doyoubi no gozen kuji ni juku ni iku yotei nan desu.*

リサ: 土曜日 の 午前 9時 に 塾に 行く 予定 なんです。

Lisa: I'm going to cram school at 9am on Saturday.

*Takuya: gogo juuniji ni yuuenchi ni ikimasen ka.*

たくや: 午後 12時 に 遊園地 に 行きません か。

Takuya: Would you like to go to the amusement park with me at 12pm?

*Lisa: juuniji wa chotto…gogo niji wa dou desu ka.*

リサ: 12時 は ちょっと。。。午後 2時 は どう です か。

Lisa: 12pm is not so convenient. How about 2pm?

*Takuya: ii desu ne!*

たくや: いい です ね!

Takuya: Sounds good!

## Lesson activities

## Sentence building

### Exercise 1

Write these times in *romaji*

1.  3:00pm *gogo sanji*
2.  10:00am *gozen juuji*
3.  8:00am *gozen hachiji*
4.  2:00pm *gogo niji*
5.  7:00am *gozen shichiji*

6.  1:00pm *gogo ichiji*
7.  9:00am *gozen kuji*
8.  11:00am *gozen juuichiji*
9.  12:00pm *gogo juuniji*
10.  4:00pm *gogo yoji*

### Exercise 2

Write these times using kanji (refer to lesson 2 for numbers).

1.  10:00pm 午後10時
2.  5:00am 午前5時
3.  7:00am 午前7時
4.  6:00pm 午後6時
5.  11:00am 午前11時

6.  2:00pm 午後2時
7.  10:00am 午前10時
8.  6:00am 午前6時
9.  12:00pm 午後12時
10.  8:00pm 午後8時

### Exercise 3

Write these times in English.

1.  *gozen ichiji* 1am
2.  *gogo hachiji* 8pm
3.  *gozen yoji* 4am
4.  *gozen rokuji* 6am
5.  *gogo niji* 2pm

6.  *gogo yoji* 4pm
7.  *gogo goji* 5pm
8.  *gogo kuji* 9pm
9.  *gozen shichiji* 7am
10.  *gozen juuichiji* 11am

### Exercise 4

Write these sentences in romaji.

1.  I wake up at 7:30am. *gozen shichijihan ni okimasu /okiru.*
2.  I play the guitar at 8:30pm. *gogo hachijihan ni gitaa wo hikimasu / hiku.*
3.  I make a lunch box at 9am. *gozen kuji ni bento wo tsukurimasu /tsukuru.*
4.  I go to work at 9:30am. *gozen kujihan ni shigoto ni ikimasu /iku.*
5.  I get on the train at 10am. *gozen juuji ni densha ni norimasu / noru.*

6. I eat lunch at 1:30pm. *gogo ichijihan ni hirugohan wo tabemasu / taberu.*

7. I go home at 7:30pm. *gogo shichiji ni ie ni kaerimasu.*

8. I go to sleep at 10:30pm. *gogo juujihan ni nemasu.*

## Exercise 5

Write these sentences in English.

1. *gozen gojihan ni okimasu.* <u>I get up at 5:30am.</u>

2. *gozen rokujihan ni asagohan wo tabemasu.* <u>I eat breakfast at 6:30am.</u>

3. *gozen kuji ni nihongo wo benkyou shimasu.* <u>I study Japanese at 9am.</u>

4. *gozen shichiji ni undou shimasu.* <u>I exercise at 7am.</u>

5. *gozen hachiji ni shigoto ni ikimasu.* <u>I go to work at 8am.</u>

6. *gozen hachijihan ni densha ni norimasu.* <u>I get on the train at 8:30am.</u>

7. *gogo sanji ni hirugohan wo tabemasu.* <u>I eat lunch at 3pm.</u>

8. *gogo shichijihan ni kaerimasu.* <u>I go home at 7:30pm.</u>

9. *gogo hachijihan ni bangohan wo tabemasu.* <u>I eat dinner at 8:30pm.</u>

10. *gozen niji ni nemasu.* <u>I go to sleep at 2am.</u>

# Appendix

**Everyday phrases**

**General phrases**

**_Listen to track 273_**

1. *hai* (はい) Yes
2. *iie* (いいえ) No
3. *konnichiwa* (こんにちは) Hello
4. *ohayou gozaimasu* (おはよう ございます) Good morning
5. *konbanwa* (こんばんは) Good evening
6. *oyasumi nasai* (おやすみ なさい) Good night
7. *jaa ne* (じゃあね) See you.
8. *mata ashita* (また 明日) See you tomorrow.
9. *moshi moshi* (もしもし) Hello (only on the phone)
10. *ogenki desu ka?* (お元気 です か) How are you?
11. *genki desu* (元気 です) I'm good.
12. *ohisashiburi desu* (お久しぶり です) Long time no see.
13. _____–*san mo?* (_____-さんも？) And you?
14. *arigatou gozaimasu* (ありがとう ございます) Thank you.
15. *douitashimashite* (どういたしまして) You're welcome.
16. *gomen nasai* (ごめんなさい) I'm sorry.
17. *sumimasen* (すみません) Excuse me.
18. *ittekimasu* (いってきます) I'm going out.
19. *itterasshai* (いってらっしゃい) Come back safely.
20. *tadaima* (ただいま) I'm back.
21. *okaeri nasai* (おかえり なさい) Welcome back.
22. *otearai wa doko desu ka* (お手洗い は どこ です か) Where is the restroom?
23. *toire wa doko desu ka* (トイレ は どこ です か) Where is the toilet?
24. *eigo ga wakarimasu ka* (英語 が 分かります か) Do you understand English?
25. *nihongo ga wakarimasen* (日本語 が 分かりません) I don't understand Japanese.
26. *nihongo sukoshi shika hanasemasen* (日本語 少し しか 話せません) I can only speak a little Japanese.

27. *sumimasen, saifu wo nakushimashita* (すみません、財布 を なくしました) Excuse me, I lost my wallet.

28. *kaban ga nusumaremashita* (鞄 が 盗まれました) My bag was stolen.

29. *sumimasen, eki wa doko desu ka* (すみません、駅 は どこ です か) Excuse me, where is the station?

30. *shashin wo totte mo ii desu ka* (写真 を 取って も いい です か) May I take a photo?

## At the store

### *Listen to track 274*

1. *irasshaimase* (いらっしゃいませ) Welcome.

2. *kore wa oikura desu ka* (これ は おいくら です か) How much is this?

3. *fukuro wo onegai shimasu* (袋 を お願い します) A bag, please.

4. *kore wo hitotsu kudasai* (これ を 一つ ください) One of these please.

5. *fooku wo onegai shimasu* (フォーク を お願い します) A fork, please.

6. *supuun wo onegai shimasu* (スプーン を お願い します) A spoon, please.

7. *o-hashi wo onegai shimasu* (お箸 を お願い します) A pair of chopsticks, please.

8. *kurejitto kaado wa tsukaemasu ka* (クレジット カード は 使えます か) May I use a credit card?

9. *PayPay wa tsukaemasu ka* (PayPay は 使えます か) May I use PayPay? *PayPay is a popular QR code payment app in Japan.

10. *genkin de onegai shimasu* (現金 で お願い します) I would like to pay in cash.

11. *atatame wo onegai shimasu* (温め を お願い します) Please heat it up. *You can have the ready-made meals heated up at the convenience store.

12. *kore to kore wo betsu no fukuro de onegai shimasu* (これ と これ を 別 の 袋 で お願い します) Please put this and this into separate bags.

13. *o-tearai wa arimasu ka* (お手洗い は あります か) Is there a bathroom here?

14. *sumimasen, ATM wa doko desu ka* (すみません、ATM は どこ です か) Excuse me, where is the ATM?

15. *reitou yasai wa doko desu ka* (冷凍 野菜 は どこ です か) Where are the frozen vegetables?

16. *shiharai houhou wa nani ga tsukaemasu ka* (支払い 方法 は 何 が 使えます か) What payment methods can be used?

## At the hospital

### *Listen to track 275*

1. *hajimete desu (*初めて です) It's my first time here.
2. *jibika no sensei no shinsetsu wo onegai shimasu (*耳鼻科 の 先生 の 診察 を お願い します) I would like to be seen by the ENT doctor, please.
3. *shinsatsuken wo wasuremashita (*診察券 を 忘れました) I forgot my patient card.
4. *hokensho wa arimasu ka* (保険証 は あります か) Do you have health insurance?
5. *okake ni natte o-machi kudasai* (おかけ に なって お待ち ください) Please take a seat.
6. *kyou wa dou shimashita ka* (今日 は どう しました か) What's the matter today?
7. *atama ga itai desu* (頭 が 痛い です) I have a headache.
8. *nodo ga itai desu* (喉 が 痛い です) My throat hurts.
9. *o-naka ga itai desu* (お腹 が 痛い です) My stomach hurts.
10. *zensoku ga arimasu* (喘息 が あります) I have asthma.
11. *kafunshou desu* (花粉症 です) I have hay fever.
12. *arerugii ga arimasu* (アレルギー が あります)  I have allergies.
13. *seki ga demasu* (咳 が 出ます) I have a cough.
14. *hanamizu ga demasu* (鼻水 が 出ます) I have a runny nose.
15. *hana ga tsumatteimasu* (鼻 が 詰まっています) I have a blocked nose.
16. *tan ga demasu* (痰 が 出ます) I have phlegm.
17. *iki ga kurushii desu* (息 が 苦しい　です) It's hard to breathe.
18. *me ga kayui desu* (目 が 痒い です) My eyes are itchy.
19. *shisshin ga arimasu* (湿疹 が あります) I have a rash.
20. *jinmashin ga arimasu* (蕁麻疹 が あります) I have hives.
21. *hifuen ga arimasu* (皮膚炎 が あります)  I have dermatitis.
22. *koshi ga itai desu* (腰 が 痛い です) My lower back hurts.
23. kata ga kotteimasu (肩 が 凝っています) My shoulders are stiff.
24. *ashikubi wo kega shimashita* (足首 を 怪我 しました) I injured my ankle.
25. *ashi wo kega shimashita* (脚 を 怪我 しました)  I injured my leg.
26. *ude wo kega shimashita* (腕 を 怪我 しました) I injured my arm.
27. *tekubi wo kega shimashita* (手首 を 怪我 しました) I injured my wrist.

28. *geri desu* (下痢 です) I have diarrhea.
29. *benpi desu* (便秘 です) I'm constipated.
30. *odaiji ni* (お大事に ) Take care. (said to a person who is sick)

## At school

### *Listen to track 276*

1. *chaimu ga narimashita* (チャイム が 鳴りました) The bell rang.
2. *chikoku shite sumimasen deshita* (遅刻 して すみません でした) 'm sorry I'm late.
3. *jugyou ga hajimarimasu* (授業 が 始まります) Class is starting.
4. *te wo agete* (手 を 上げて) Raise your hand.
5. *kyoukasho wo hiraite* (教科書 を 開いて) Open your textbook.
6. *kyoukasho wo tojite* (教科書 を 閉じて) Close your textbook.
7. *enpitsu wo hirotte* (鉛筆 を 拾って) Pick up your pencil.
8. *enpitsu wo otoshimashita yo* (鉛筆 を 落としました よ) You dropped your pencil.
9. *bunbougu wo katadzukete* (文房具 を 片付けて) Tidy up your stationery.
10. *fudebako wo wasuremashita* (筆箱 を 忘れました) I forgot your pencil case.
11. *enpitsu wo wasuremashita* (鉛筆 を 忘れました) I forgot my pencil.
12. *kyoukasho wo wasuremashita* (教科書 を 忘れました) I forgot my textbook.
13. *shukudai wo wasuremashita* (宿題 を 忘れました) I forgot my homework.
14. *ongaku kyoushitsu ga mitsukeraremasen* (音楽 教室 が 見つけられません) I can't find the music room.
15. *hokenshitsu ni ikitai* (保健室 に 行きたい です) I want to go to the nurse's office.
16. *pen wo karite mo ii desu ka* (ペン を 借りて も いい です か) May I borrow a pen?
17. *kami wo moratte mo ii desu ka* (紙 を 貰って も いい です か) May I have a piece of paper?
18. *otearai ni itte mo ii desu ka* (お手洗い に 行って も いい です か) May I go to the bathroom?
19. *watashi no rokkaa ni haitte imasu* (私 の ロッカー に 入っています) It's in my locker.
20. *tesuto wa itsu desu ka* (テスト は いつ です か) When is the test?
21. *kono shitsumon ga wakarimasen* (この 質問 が 分かりません) I don't understand this question.

22. *wakarimasen* (分かりません) I don't understand. / I don't know.

23. *sansuu no shiken ga arimasu* (算数 の 試験 が あります) I have a math exam.

24. *o-bentou wo mottekimashita* (お弁当 を 持ってきました) I brought a lunch box.

## At the station

### *Listen to track 277*

1. *kippu wo kaitai desu* (切符 を 買いたい です) I want to buy a ticket.

2. *kippu no kounyuu no shikata ga wakarimasen* (切符 の 購入 の 仕方 が 分かりません) I don't know how to buy a ticket.

3. *kenbaiki wa doko desu ka* (券売機 は どこ です か) Where is the ticket machine?

4. *SUICA wo kaitai desu* (SUICAを買いたいです) I would like to buy a SUICA* card.

5. *PASMO wo kaitai desu* (PASMOを買いたいです) I would like to buy a PASMO* card. *SUICA and PASMO are chargeable transportation IC cards.

6. *teikiken wo tsukuritai desu* (定期券を作りたいです) I would like to make a commuter pass. *A commuter pass is a card which allows you to use a specific route for 1 month, 3 months, or 6 months. This is generally your route to work or to school.

7. *Akihabara eki yuki no densha wa dore desu ka* (秋葉原 行き の 電車 は どれ です か) Which train is bound for Akihabara?

8. *Harajuku yuki no shuuden wa nanji desu ka* (原宿 行き の 終電 は 何時 です か) What time is the last train for Harajuku?

9. *kono densha wa Shibuya ni tomarimasu ka* (この 電車 は 渋谷 に 止まります か) Does this train stop at Shibuya?

10. *sumimasen, chigau kippu wo katteshimaimashita* (すみません、違う切符 を 買ってしまいました) Excuse me, I bought the wrong ticket.

11. *sumimasen, toukyou eki ni ikitai n desu ga, nanban hoomu desu ka* (すみません 東京駅に行きたいんですが、何番ホームですか) Excuse me, I would like to go to Tokyo station. Which platform is it?

12. *sumimasen, yonban hoomu ga mitsukerarenai n desu* (すみません、4番ホームが見つけられないんです) Excuse me, but I can't find platform 4.

13. *douzo suwattekudasai* (どうぞ座ってください) Please take a seat.

14. *keitai wo senro ni otoshimashita* (携帯を線路に落としました) I dropped my cell phone on the tracks.

15. *kaisatsu wa doko ni arimasu ka* (改札はどこにありますか) Where is the ticket gate?

16. *honjitsu wa densha wa mou arimasen* (本日 は 電車 は もう ありません) The trains have stopped running for today.

17. *okomari deshou ka* (お困り でしょう か) Do you need help?

18. *kyuukou no hou ga hayai desu* (急行 の 方 が 早い です) The express train is faster.

19. *kakueki wa Suidoubashi eki ni tomarimasu* (各駅 は 水道橋 駅 に 止まります) The local train stops at Suidobashi station.

20. *tokkyuu wa Narita kuukou ni tomarimasu.* (特急 は 成田 空港 に 止まります) The limited express stops at Narita Airport.

## At the hotel

### Listen to track 278

1. *yoyaku ga arimasu* (予約 が あります) I have a reservation.

2. *chekkuin wo onegai shimasu* (チェックインをお願いします) I would like to check in, please.

3. *pasupooto no kopii wo totte mo yoroshii deshou ka* (パスポートのコピーを取ってもよろしいでしょうか) May I take a copy of your passport?

4. *hai, yoroshiku onegai shimasu* (はい、よろしくお願いします) Yes, please.

5. *yoyaku ga arimasen* (予約がありません) I don't have a reservation.

6. *hitori beya wo yoyaku shitaidesu* (一人部屋予約をしたいです) I would like to reserve a room for one.

7. *hitori beya wo onegai shimasu* (一人部屋をお願いします) A room for one, please.

8. *futari beya wo onegai shimasu* (二人部屋をお願いします) A room for two, please.

9. *kitsuen no heya wo onegai shimasu* (喫煙の部屋をお願いします) A smoking room, please.

10. *kinen no heya wo onegai shimasu* (禁煙の部屋をお願いします) A non-smoking room.

11. *tsuin beddo wo onegai shimasu* (ツインベッドをお願いします) I'd like a twin bed, please.

12. *daburu beddo wo onegai shimasu* (ダブルベッドをお願いします) I'd like a double bed, please.

13. *chekkuauto wa nanji desu ka* (チェックアウト は 何時 です か) What time is checkout?

14. *Wi-Fi wa arimasu ka* (Wi-Fi は　あります　か) Is there Wi-Fi?

15. *kinko wa arimasu ka* (金庫　は　あります　か) Is there a safe?

16. *airon wa arimasu ka* (アイロン　は　あります　か) Is there air conditioning?

17. *hea doraiyaa wa arimasu ka* (ヘア　ドライヤー　は　あります　か) Is there a hairdryer?

18. *ATM wa arimasu ka* (ATM は　あります　か) Is there an ATM?

19. *ryougae dekimasu ka* (両替　できます　か) Could I get some change?

20. *asagohan wa nanji desu ka* (朝ご飯は何時ですか？) What time is breakfast?

21. *kagi wo onegai shimasu* (鍵　を　お願い　します) Key, please.

22. *takushii wo onegai shimasu* (タクシー　を　お願い　します) A taxi, please.

23. *ruumu saabisu wo onegai shimasu* (ルーム　サービス　を　お願い　します) Room service, please.

24. *ichiban chikai izakaya wa doko desu ka* (一番　近い　居酒屋　は　どこ　です　か) Where is the nearest bar?

25. *ichiban chikai konbini wa doko desu ka* (一番　近い　コンビニ　は　どこ　です　か) Where is the nearest convenience store?

26. *heya ni kite kudasai* (部屋　に　来て　ください) Please come to my room.

27. *danbou ga tsukaemasen* (暖房　が　使えません) The heater doesn't work.

28. *eakon ga tsukaemasen* (エアコン　が　使えません) The air conditioner doesn't work.

29. *shawaa ga tsukaemasen* (シャワー　が　使えません) The shower doesn't work.

30. *chekkuauto wo onegai shimasu* (チェック　アウト　を　お願いします) I'd like to check out, please.

31. *nimotsu wo azukeraremasu ka* (荷物　を　預けられます　か) Could you look after my/our luggage.

32. *kusuri wo heya ni wasuremashita* (薬　を　部屋　に　忘れました) I forgot my medication in the room.

## At the restaurant

### Listen to track 279

1. *nanmei-sama desu ka* (何名様　です　か) How many people?
2. *futari desu* (二人　です) Two people
3. *kitsuenseki wo onegai shimasu* (喫煙席　を　お願い　します) A smoking seat, please.
4. *kinenseki wo onegai shimasu* (禁煙席　を　お願い　します) A non-smoking seat please.
5. *yoyaku ga arimasu* (予約　が　あります) I have a reservation.
6. *menyuu wo onegai shimasu* (メニュー　を　お願い　します) A menu, please.
7. *eigo no menyuu wa arimasu ka* (英語　の　メニュー　は　あります　か) Do you have an English menu?
8. *nonarukooru no biiru wa arimasu ka* (ノンアルコール　の　ビール　は　あります　か) Do you have non-alcoholic beer?
9. *osusume wa nan desu ka* (おすすめ　は　何　です　か) What do you recommend?
10. *kore wa nan desu ka* (これ　は　何　です　か) What is this?
11. *mou ichido ii desu ka* (もう　一度　いい　です　か) Could you say that again please?
12. *kore wo onegai shimasu* (これ　を　お願い　します) I'll have this, please.
13. *kore wo kudasai* (これ　を　ください) I'll have this, please.
14. *kore wo futatsu kudasai* (これ　を　二つ　ください) Two of these, please.
15. *onaji no onegai shimasu* (同じ　の　お願い　します) I'll have the same, please.
16. *tamanegi nuki dekimasu ka* (玉ねぎ　抜き　できます　か) Could I have it without onions?
17. *omizu futatsu onegai shimasu* (お水　二つ　お願い　します) Two glasses of water, please.
18. *oishii desu* (美味しい　です) It's delicious.
19. *okaikei wo onegai shimasu* (お会計　を　お願いします) The bill, please.
20. *okaikei wo betsubetsu ni dekimasu ka* (お会計　を　別々　に　できます　か) Could we pay separately?
21. *gochisousama deshita* (ご馳走様　でした) Thank you for the meal.

# Conclusion

Learning grammar is never an easy task, so if you were able to finish all the lessons in this book by consistently learning everyday, kudos to you. You did an amazing job, and you should be very happy with your achievement.

If you were not able to follow the daily schedules recommended, don't despair. The important thing is you made use of this book to build a solid foundation for your Japanese grammar. We hope that you will continue to keep learning everyday.

Even just an hour a day or less will go a long way. It could be just listening to a 30-minute Japanese podcast, watching a Japanese movie or TV series, writing to a friend in Japan, talking to a native Japanese speaker, changing your social media settings to Japanese or reading the news in Japanese ... the list goes on.

If you wish to further your studies in Japanese language, we have other books available at Talk in Japanese and on Amazon. Please feel free to browse the different titles. Books such as Japanese Short Stories will help improve your reading and listening skills as well as solidify the knowledge you have learned in this grammar book.

Thank you so much for using this book. It has been a great 17 days (or more) with you. We wish you the best of luck in your Japanese studies.

I'd love to hear from you! Would it be too much to ask what you think about this book? If you can spare a few minutes, do let me know your thoughts by sending an email to support@talkinjapanese.com or leaving a review and rating on Amazon would be great as well.


Thank you,

Frederic Bibard

Founder, Talk in Japanese

# How to Download the Audio

Please take note that the audio are in MP3 format and need to be accessed online. No worries though; it's quite easy!

On your computer, smartphone, iphone/ipad or tablet, simply go to this link:

https://talkinjapanese.com/grammar-beginner-audio/

Do you have any problems downloading the audio? If you do, feel free to send an email to support@talkinjapanese.com. We'll do our best to assist you, but we would greatly appreciate if you could thoroughly review the instructions first.

Thank you,

Frederic Bibard

Founder, Talk in Japanese

28713414R00160